The Federal
Reserve System

ALSO BY DONALD R. WELLS

The Race for the Governor's Cup:
The Pacific Coast League Playoffs, 1936–1954
(McFarland, 2000)

The Federal Reserve System

A History

Donald R. Wells

McFarland & Company, Inc., Publishers
Jefferson, North Carolina, and London

LIBRARY OF CONGRESS CATALOGUING-IN-PUBLICATION DATA

Wells, Donald R., 1932–
    The Federal Reserve system : a history / Donald R. Wells.
      p.   cm.
    Includes bibliographical references and index.

    ISBN 0-7864-1880-X (softcover : 50# alkaline paper) ∞

    1. Federal Reserve banks.   2. Board of Governors of the
Federal Reserve System (U.S.)   I. Title.
HG2563.W3626   2004
332.1'1'0973 — dc22   2004014714

British Library cataloguing data are available

Manufactured in the United States of America

Cover image ©2003 Digital Vision

*McFarland & Company, Inc., Publishers
  Box 611, Jefferson, North Carolina 28640
   www.mcfarlandpub.com*

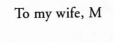

To my wife, M

Contents

Contents

Preface

This book is intended for the general public. It has been my experience in teaching money and banking for over 30 years that most people know very little about the Federal Reserve, why it came into being, how it functions, and that the decisions it makes are independent of both the president and the Congress. It is my hope that the book will help people understand how monetary decisions affect the economy.

The Federal Reserve Act was passed in December 1913, but the Fed did not begin operations until November 1914. The reason for passage of this act was the recurrence of banking panics in which the public was unable to convert bank deposits into currency on demand. The framers of the Federal Reserve Act wanted an outside source of currency and bank reserves. They hoped that such reserves would prevent bank panics by allowing the money supply to increase when it was needed for business expansion and then contract when no longer needed. This theory, called the "real bills doctrine," has been rejected by modern economic theory. The reasons U.S. banks could not issue all the currency the public wanted at particular times were the many restrictions on the issuance of national bank notes and the ban against state chartered banks issuing any notes. No such problem existed in Canada. This book will show that a major panic was averted in 1914 after World War I broke out in Europe when U.S. national banks were allowed to issue a special emergency currency.

In order to sell the American public and Congress on the establishment of the Fed, the framers of the act had to convince them that this was not going to be a central bank and that it would not violate the gold standard. Therefore, instead of having one central location in either New York or Washington, the act provided for twelve regional Federal Reserve Banks plus a board in Washington. This led to a struggle for control which was not settled until the Banking Act of 1935 placed the power with the board. Throughout the 1920s and early 1930s, there were struggles for dominance by the New York Federal Reserve Bank and the board in Washington. This conflict intensified after the Fed discovered a new tool, open market operations, that allowed the Fed to add new reserves to the system by buying government bonds, rather than passively waiting for commercial banks to come to a district Federal Reserve Bank and borrow by discounting commercial paper as the Federal Reserve Act specified.

When the leader of the New York Fed, Benjamin Strong, died in 1928, the Fed was left without a dominant personality to guide it through the worst part of the Great Depression. The Fed failed completely to fulfill its role as a lender of last resort in that period. There was no direction coming out of the board in Washington, and most of the regional Federal Reserve Banks worried more about their own balance sheets than the well-being of the commercial banks. The money supply contracted by one-third (33%) as 9,000 banks failed from 1929 to 1933. Before the Fed had been established, banks that were solvent but illiquid had been allowed to remain open and clear checks. In contrast, illiquid banks were closed in the 1929–1933 period, causing contagious bank runs. Many observers pointed out how much better off we had been when the emergency currency was used in the 1914 crisis.

Under the New Deal and World War II, the Fed became a passive institution, taking a back seat to the Treasury. The one exception was when the Fed doubled the reserve requirements of banks in 1936 and 1937, which caused a large contraction and stifled a weak recovery. But once the war started, the Fed was relegated to supporting the prices of government bonds, which meant they could not use their main tool of open market operations.

After World War II was over, the country did not experience a return to the Depression as some feared, but instead embarked on a period of prosperity. The Fed wanted to use its ability to control inflation by selling government bonds in the open market. The Treasury, on the other hand, wanted the Fed to continue to support bond prices at par, so that the Treasury could keep borrowing at 2.5 per cent and bond holders would not suffer any capital losses. This conflict heated up after the Korean War began in June 1950, because inflation was becoming a problem. However, President Truman wanted the Fed to continue supporting these bonds to keep interest rates low. In 1951, the Treasury and the Fed finally reached an accord that permitted the Fed to use open market operations even though some long-term government bonds would fall in price. In 1953, the Fed felt it could finally engage in an independent monetary policy, which it did by only buying and selling short term Treasury bills, to avoid being trapped in another bond support program.

The leader of the Fed in this period from 1951 to 1970 was William McChesney Martin. It was he who set up the "bills only" policy in the 1950s, but he was persuaded to abandon it in the early 1960s. But when the Vietnam War was raging, Martin had a major conflict with President Johnson about the conduct of monetary policy. Johnson wanted an easy money policy to prevent rising interest rates from choking off private spending, but Martin feared inflation. It was after the Fed buckled that inflation became chronic, lasting from the late 1960s to the early 1980s.

The severe inflation that lasted over 15 years caused (1) the abandonment of the gold reserve requirements to which the Federal Reserve had been subjected; (2) the breakdown of the fixed exchange rate system that had been set up in 1944; (3) high nominal interest rates that exceeded what banks and financial intermediaries could pay, causing the public to pull its funds from these institutions and seek higher rates in the direct financial market; (4)the ill-fated imposition of wage and price controls by the Nixon Administration in 1971. Along with severe inflation, the nation experienced high unemployment in 1974 and 1975; the combination was called "stagflation." The Fed was unable to combat one problem without making the other worse. During the late 1970s, economists argued that only unexpected inflation could lower unemployment, and then only until the public came to expect the inflation and to demand cost-of-living escalator clauses in its wage contracts.

In late 1979, Paul Volcker became chairman of the Federal Reserve Board. It was Volcker who was willing to withstand the criticism of a tight money policy that finally brought down the inflation by breaking the public's expectations of continually rising prices. Unemployment reached 10 per cent in 1982, but the public finally realized that the Fed was serious about ending inflation. In 1980 a major congressional act gave the Fed what it had been seeking since it began: control over all the nation's banks. The Fed could set reserve requirements for all institutions that offered checkable deposits, and no ceiling would be placed on what financial institutions could pay on their deposits. But this law also made it difficult for the Fed to control the money supply, because the public now was holding both savings and transaction balances in the same account since interest could be earned on these accounts.

During the latter part of Volcker's eight-year term, newly appointed members of the Board of Governors wanted an easier money policy than did Chairman Volcker. This was one factor in Volcker stepping down and being replaced by Alan Greenspan. Greenspan immediately had to deal with a severe drop in the stock market and a major crisis caused by the failure of many savings and loan associations. This required another major congressional act and the subsequent buildup of bank and savings association insurance funds, which was accomplished by the mid–1990s. Another feature of both the Volcker and Greenspan eras has been the dominance of professional economists on the Board of Governors and also as presidents of the district Federal Reserve Banks. This was a major departure from the 1960s when Chairman William McChesney Martin objected to having too many economists on the board. Under Greenspan, voting on monetary policy by the Open Market Committee has often been unanimous even when several members were appointed by a president of the opposite political party. This in all probability is because of the hard lesson learned during the chronic inflation of the 1970s: an easy money policy does not reduce unemployment but does create inflation.

The most helpful sources were the scholarly works of Milton Friedman and Anna Schwartz including *The Monetary History of the United States 1867–1960* and A. H. Meltzer's *A History of the Federal Reserve,* Volume 1. (Volume 1 goes to 1951; Volume 2 is not out at this writing.) Other valuable sources were Robert Degan's *The American Monetary System* and *A Biographical Dictionary of the Board of Governors of the Federal Reserve System* edited by Bernard Katz. Other sources included various Federal Reserve Bulletins and annual reports of the Federal Deposit Insurance Corporation.

1

U.S. Banking before the Federal Reserve

Before the Civil War of 1861–1865, all banks in the U.S. were chartered by state governments except for the two United States Banks, which were chartered by the federal government for twenty years each. Both of these United States Banks performed some central bank functions while simultaneously acting as regular commercial banks. The First United States bank was chartered in 1791 during George Washington's administration and was strongly supported by his secretary of the treasury, Alexander Hamilton, but opposed by Secretary of State Thomas Jefferson. This bank had a capital of $10 million, of which $2 million was subscribed by the federal government. Its main office was in Philadelphia but it had branches in most American cities, unlike state banks that usually had no branches or branched only within their home state. This quasi-government bank acted as the government's fiscal agent, dealt in gold bullion and foreign exchange, and invested in government bonds. But it also made loans to private businesses, competing with private state banks. The bank notes of this institution were given legal tender status, meaning they had to be accepted in payment for debts. State banks also issued bank notes but theirs were not legal tender, so state banks often used the notes of the First United States Bank for reserves and converted their own bank notes into the notes of the U.S. bank. But its charter was not renewed in 1811 because most state banks resented the competition and

7

Democratic Republican party, opposed it, including president James Madison.

The U.S. fought its second war with England from 1812 to 1814 without a federally chartered bank. Between 1811 and 1814, about 120 new bank charters were granted by the various states, and many of them made loans to the federal government for the war. However, their excessive note issues often led to suspensions of payment in specie, causing their bank notes to circulate at various discounts. This chaotic situation helped spur the Congress to establish a Second United States Bank in 1816. This bank had $35 million in capital, of which $7 million was subscribed by the federal government. All this bank's deposits as well as bank notes were legal tender. Again, state banks redeemed their notes in this bank's notes, but state banks resented it when the United States bank would present their notes for payment in specie. State banks, however, got the United States bank to agree to contribute its resources to any state bank in an emergency where its credit was endangered. This was an agreement to become a lender of last resort, a function that modern central banks perform.

Like its predecessor, the Second United States Bank incurred the wrath of state banks because it restricted their expansion by presenting their notes for payment in either specie or United States banknotes. It also annoyed farmers who wanted easier credit and states' rights advocates who believed the federal government was usurping powers that belonged to the states. But, most of all, it annoyed president Andrew Jackson, who vehemently opposed its existence. He removed all the government deposits from this bank and put them in various state banks. He also vetoed its request for an extension of its twenty-year charter, and the bank ceased to exist after 1836.

A severe financial panic began in 1837, and hard times lasted for several years. That year the federal government issued its "Specie Circular," which directed land agents to accept only specie or bank notes that were readily convertible into specie in payment for public lands. This led to a contraction of bank notes and deposits. Bank failures and suspensions of cash payments were common. When some of the state banks that held federal government deposits failed, it led to the establishment of an Independent Treasury System, wherein the Treasury kept its funds in its own vaults and in various sub-treasuries around the country. When receipts and expenditures of the government were small, this system was adequate, but it had to be modified during the Civil War.

One area of the country that had few suspensions of cash payments by banks was New England because of the Suffolk System. In other areas of the country, bank notes often failed to return to the issuing bank because there was no branching beyond state lines. The less the chance of notes being sent home for redemption, the greater the opportunity of the bank to over issue. But the Suffolk Bank in Boston in 1818, by strength of its position, got the country banks in New England to agree to each hold $5000 permanently in a deposit at the Suffolk Bank, plus an additional amount to redeem their notes that reached Boston. If the country banks refused, the Suffolk Bank would gather its notes and immediately present them for payment in specie. But if the country bank complied, its notes would be received at par. By 1825, most of the New England banks were members of this system.

One of the main problems of the American banking system was its lack of nationwide branching. This led to a very large number and variety of distinctive bank notes, making it difficult for the public to keep up with the value of each because many circulated at a discount. Counterfeiting was also rampant with so many types of notes. Moreover, various merchants and brokers took it upon themselves to buy up bank notes far from the issuer at a large discount, and then put them out close to home where there might be no discount or a very small one. Banknote reports were published to try to keep the public informed about the value of bank notes. The lack of branching also prevented banks from diversifying their loan portfolios, particularly in agricultural states.

Another problem with the American banking system before the Civil War was that in many cases, a state would force any bank operating within it boundaries to buy a significant amount of bonds from that state government. This was true if the banks were chartered, or if they operated under the so-called "free banking" laws. There was opposition to chartering of banks because many felt that this was a privilege requiring a special act of the state legislature that only the well-connected could acquire. So several states, beginning with New York in 1838, passed laws that allowed banks to start without an act of the legislature if the owners of the bank deposited with the state an amount of specie, or notes of banks convertible into specie, to purchase state government bonds, which would limit the amount of notes the bank could issue. In any case, banks were forced to buy these state government bonds, which later might fall in value. Holding these state bonds often prevented banks from making profitable loans to business firms.

Because many holders of bank notes in the pre–Civil War era were unable to keep up on their value, six states tried to protect them with note guarantee schemes. Note protection was provided either by banks paying assessments to an insurance fund, by banks mutually guaranteeing the notes of a failed bank, or by a combination of the two. Banks in New York, Vermont and Michigan paid into an insurance fund; Indiana used the mutual guarantee in which banks were assessed enough to pay the notes of a failed bank; Ohio and Iowa had the combined plan that called for immediate payment of note holders through assessment of banks and later reimbursement of the banks by the fund.

New York's plan began in 1829 but insured both notes and deposits. After 1842, the fund was depleted and thereafter covered only bank notes. The comptroller of New York did not close failed banks during that troubled year, but redeemed the notes from the safety fund. These troubled banks later made good that amount. After that panicky year of 1842, the state of New York acquired the right to sell bonds to meet insurance claims, and the banks' payments into the fund redeemed the bonds.

Michigan had the worst experience because its plan began during the panic of 1837, when specie payments were suspended. When specie payments were resumed in 1838, little had been paid into the fund, so the scheme collapsed with no one being reimbursed.

Vermont's plan began in 1831 and was able to pay only one-third of its claims because the fund was depleted by the banks who withdrew from the plan.

Indiana had the best experience. Its plan began in 1834 with the mutual guarantee system. Payment would not be made until the failed bank's assets were liquidated, but this redemption would be 100 percent. No failures occurred, owing to the excellent supervision of banks — supervision chosen by bankers and not by politicians.

Ohio's plan began in 1845 and also reimbursed note holders 100 percent. Failing banks were kept open to keep money circulating by a plan in which the state held the notes of a bank in trouble and allowed deposits to be drawn on that amount. The plan began with a large fund, and member banks were assessed after a failure. The supervisors were chosen by bankers.

Iowa's plan began in 1858 and started with a fund large enough to redeem notes 100 percent. As with Indiana, no special assessment was needed and the inspectors were chosen by bankers.

Congress, acting under powers given by the Constitution, passed a Coinage Act in 1792 that defined silver as 371.25 grains per ounce and gold as 24.75 grains per ounce. This meant that gold was 15 times as valuable as silver, but in Europe the markets valued gold at 16 times silver. This caused the U.S. to lose gold and acquire a great deal of silver, because each metal flowed to where it could command the highest price.

To rectify the above discrepancy, in 1834 Congress passed the Gold Bill, which reduced the grains of gold from 24.75 per ounce to 23.20. In 1837, the gold was changed slightly to 23.22 grains per ounce, making the mint price of gold $20.67 per ounce and silver $1.29 per ounce. This ratio was more in line with other countries. In 1853, Congress allowed fractional silver coins, but their silver content was reduced by 7 percent so they would be more valuable as a coin than as a commodity. Finally, in 1857 all laws making foreign coins legal tender were repealed.

The Civil War caused a major change in the American banking system. The national government borrowed specie from the northern banks while it simultaneously issued $150 million in greenbacks, which were nonredeemable in specie but were legal tender for all debts except for duties on imports or interest on the public debt. Two further issues of this fiat money followed, making a total of $450 million. Fiat money is paper currency not redeemable in specie. The gold standard was suspended and not resumed until 1879. But the federal government needed more money to fight the Civil War. So it copied what state governments had been doing; it established national banks under a bond deposit system.

The National Bank Act allowed the formation of a new bank if at least five principals could accumulate capital of at least $50,000. Before this bank could issue bank notes, it had to secure them by depositing a special issue of 2 percent government bonds with the new office of the Comptroller of the Currency in Washington. The new national bank notes were printed by the Bureau of Engraving in Washington and were uniform in appearance. These notes could not exceed 90 percent of the market value of the bonds deposited. Shareholders of these national banks had double liability. In addition to backing their notes with government bonds, the banks had to have cash reserves in either gold or greenbacks to back their deposits. This law was designed not only to sell government bonds to finance the war, but also to replace the various state bank notes with a uniform currency.

The national bank system did not correct the shortcomings of the pre–Civil War banking system. All national banks were unit banks except for those state banks that took out national charters; those state banks were allowed to keep their intrastate branches. Banknotes could not be issued against all a bank's assets, but only against these government bonds. The volume of bank notes thus became a function of the profitability of holding 2 percent government bonds, and not of the public's desired asset ratio of currency to deposits. To give national banks the sole right to issue bank notes, a 10 percent tax was levied on state bank notes. The National Bank Act required all national banks to accept each other's notes at par. This was to overcome the problem experienced with the pre–Civil War state bank notes, which often circulated at a discount when they were far from the point of issuance.

It was cumbersome to expand or contract these national bank notes. The special issue government bonds had to be purchased by a national bank in the open market and then deposited with the Comptroller in Washington before the national bank received the new notes. These bank notes could not be retired until the need for them had passed, so many banks never bothered to issue notes. Up until 1908, only $3 million in bank notes per month could be retired, but after that the figure rose to $9 million. Many national banks charged their borrowers more if they wanted to take their loan funds in bank notes rather than in a deposit. Between 1882 and 1891, national banks reduced their note issue by $185.9 million, possibly because the national debt was being retired. Those 2 percent bonds rose above par; that is, banks would have to pay more than $1000 for a $1000 bond. Between 1875 and 1900, national banks never issued more than 30 percent of the allowable amount of bank notes.

This changed after 1900, because the law allowed national banks to issue bank notes up to 100 percent of the par value of their bonds. After the gold discovery in Alaska in the late 1890s, the price level rose after falling for over 25 years. There was a greater demand for currency on the part of the public, so the amount of bank notes held by the public increased from $323.5 million in 1900 to $733.7 million in 1914. The public's holding of currency rose with the rising price level, but the inability of national banks to expand and contract their notes on demand led to currency hoarding, bank suspensions, and a premium on currency in a crisis.

State banks continued to operate alongside national banks, but state banks could not issue bank notes. However, they created deposits in the lending process and could use any currency (gold, greenbacks or national bank notes), for reserves, whereas national banks could not use national bank notes as a reserve for their deposits. In many cases, state banks were smaller than national banks and often were allowed to begin with much lower capital. By 1913, there were about 13,000 state-chartered banks in the U.S. compared to 7,000 national banks.

National banks also had to hold cash reserves for their deposits, and these cash reserves had to be in the form of lawful money, which consisted of gold, gold certificates or greenbacks — not national bank notes. Greenbacks, which were fixed at $347 million, were left over from financing the Civil War. National banks outside the central reserve cities of New York, Chicago and St. Louis could hold part of their reserves as a deposit in the central reserve city banks, but the latter had to hold all 25 percent of their reserves in vault cash. Banks in reserve cities had a 25 percent reserve requirement against their deposits, but half of that could be held on deposit in the central reserve cities. Country banks had to hold 15 percent reserves against their deposits, but only 6 percent had to be in their vaults. The other 9 percent could be on deposit in a reserve city bank. These cash reserves were a frozen asset that could not be used in a crisis. This pyramiding of reserves made bank runs contagious because each bank had to think of itself first when faced with a demand for cash, and consequently would pull its deposits from the large city bank.

State-chartered banks, while not allowed to issue bank notes, could use national bank notes as well as any currency for their reserves. In 1873, state banks held deposits equal to 67 percent of the deposits in national banks, but by 1901 their deposits were 145 percent of national bank deposits. This growth created greater demand for currency throughout the country, but these state banks could only meet the increased demand for cash by paying out their most liquid asset, vault cash. On the other hand, if a national bank had any of its own notes that had not been issued, it could exchange them for deposits without draining its cash reserves. By contrast, Canadian banks, which could branch all over the country, could issue their bank notes without having to back them with any specific asset. such as a government bond. Consequently, they rarely faced the panics experienced by the United States.

This difference made by being able to issue bank notes is illustrated below:

State Chartered Bank		National Bank or Canadian Bank	
Assets	*Liabilities*	*Assets*	*Liabilities*
-Vault Cash	- Deposits	No Change	+ Banknotes
			- Deposits

In October 1907, a panic occurred which caused banks to suspend cash payments. The catalyst for this panic was the failure of the Knickerbocker Trust Company in New York City. These trust companies had a competitive advantage over banks because they did not have to hold any fixed amount of cash reserve, could lend on real estate, and could trade stocks and bonds. These trusts in New York were able to increase their deposits from $198 million in 1898 to $834 million in 1906. In 1903, when the New York Clearinghouse Association ruled that all member trust companies had to hold 10 percent cash reserves, most of them dropped their membership, which required banks to send messengers to clear checks rather than have it done through the clearinghouse. The fact that trust companies could draw business away from banks by offering higher interest on deposits and lower charges for other services, while relying on bank loans for liquidity, caused resentment among the large banks. Wealthy financier J. P. Morgan organized a money pool of $25 million to lend to trust companies, but the New York banks were slow to lend to the trusts because the banks were faced with huge demands for cash withdrawals from all the banks around the country that had deposited reserve funds with them. In just five weeks, New York banks lost $51 million of vault cash. Some national banks did increase their issue of bank notes, but new national bank notes took some time before they could be put in the hands of the eager public.

Four days after the failure of the Knickerbocker Trust Company, the New York Clearinghouse Association met to arrange the issuance of clearinghouse loan certificates (a forerunner of today's federal funds market), which allowed banks needing liquidity to borrow from those who had surplus funds. These loan certificates, which were used in the panics of 1873 and 1893, could be used as a settlement medium that actually increased the total reserves in the system. But the mere issuance of these loan certificates signaled to the country that there was a serious liquidity crisis, which caused banks around the country to withdraw more funds from their New York correspondent banks. Country banks withdrew cash to pay their depositors but also hoarded more cash reserve than required. These interior banks were holding $47.6 million more in cash reserves, but their reserve deposits in New York banks fell by $54 million.

This pressure on the New York banks caused them to look to the U.S. Treasury for assistance. Secretary of the Treasury Leslie Shaw, in the Theodore Roosevelt administration, bought $36 million of government bonds from the New York banks, hoping to stem the panic. The Independent Treasury System was still in operation but it relaxed its rules when a crisis occurred. The Treasury was thus acting as a central bank, but it was unable to stop the excessive demand for currency.

This was a major factor in the drive for a permanent agency that could supply additional reserves to the banking system. But in 1907, market forces had to work without much government help to end the panic. This was accomplished by very high interest rates on short-term loans in the New York money market, which attracted an inflow of over $100 million in gold from Europe. In addition, the currency shortage caused a 4 percent premium on currency, which helped draw it out of hoards. This premium kept dropping as more banks and department stores took advantage of the profit by giving up the currency they had been hoarding in safe deposit boxes for checking book money. The premium dropped from 4 percent in the second week of November to only ⅛ of 1 percent in late December.

Many cities in the United States experienced the issuance of an illegal but accepted currency through their clearinghouses. These were issued in small denominations and served as hand-to-hand currency, even though they were in violation of the law from the 1860s that put a 10 percent tax on all bank notes not issued by national banks. In addition, Canadian bank notes circulated in American cities. But this experience convinced many political leaders and New York bankers that some reform was needed in the banking system.

The panic of 1907 served as a clear sign that the American banking system needed reform. Politicians had blamed previous panics on external factors. The suspension of cash payments in 1873 was blamed on the uncertainty regarding the resumption of specie payments, while the 1893 suspension was often attributed to the repeal of the Sherman Silver Purchase Act. In each of those years, the economy was depressed and the price level was falling. But in 1907, no external factor could be blamed. Prices in general were rising from the major gold discovery in Alaska in 1898. In addition, the provisions regarding the issuance of national bank notes had been relaxed in 1900, allowing them to be issued to the full value, rather than 90 percent, of the government bonds held for that purpose. Moreover, most of the government debt was refunded into 2 percent, 30 year bonds that were eligible for issue. Yet, even though the absolute amount of bank notes had increased sharply since 1900, banks still had to resort to the use of clearing house loan certificates, and had to suspend cash payments in 1907.

In 1908, Congress passed the Aldrich Vreeland Act. It permitted any ten or more national banks with an aggregate capital of at least $5 million to form national currency associations to issue bank notes that could be backed by almost any securities the banks were holding, not just government bonds. The national currency association officers were to approve the securities deposited with it, and were then to apply to the Comptroller of the Currency for delivery of the bank notes. The Treasury had a lien, not only on the deposited securities, but also on all of the assets of the banks comprising the currency association. The banks in the currency association were all liable for any emergency currency issued. But a tax of 5 percent per year was to be placed on this issue for the first month it was outstanding. This tax was to be increased by 1 percentage point per year for each month this emergency currency was outstanding, until a maximum of 10 percent per year was reached. This tax may have been the reason no bank notes were issued under this law for six years, or there may not have been a need for it. The provisions of this act were to expire on June 30, 1914, because the act also authorized the creation of a National Monetary Commission to study the problems of the American monetary system and to recommend changes.

Senator Nelson Aldrich chaired the commission, which consisted of nine senators and nine members of the House of Representatives. Aldrich selected two experts to advise the commission: Paul Warburg, a German-born investment banker; and Henry Davison, a partner of J. P. Morgan. Warburg was extremely influential, being a strong advocate of a central bank based on the German model. In late 1910, a secret meeting of those advocating a central bank met in Jekyll Island, Georgia, to draft a bill for a central bank. Besides Warburg, Davison and Aldrich, others at the meeting were Frank Vanderlip of the National City Bank, Charles Norton of the First National Bank of New York, and Professor A. Piatt Andrew of Harvard. Most of the work was Warburg's; he wanted to disguise the idea of a central bank by having decentralized regional banks. This draft was presented to the National Monetary Commission as the Aldrich Bill. It called for a National Reserve Association, which would be one centralized bank with fifteen branches around the country. The board members in Washington were to be chosen by the influential banks. With this arrangement, there would be only one discount rate all over the nation. The central bank would set the reserve requirements.

After many political compromises, the end result was the Federal Reserve Act passed on December 23, 1913. A major political change was also involved. The commission began its work in the last year of Theodore Roosevelt's administration and continued under fellow Republican William Howard Taft. But the Democrats won both houses of Congress in the mid-term election of 1910. Then in 1912, the Democrats not only kept both houses of Congress but also won the White House with Woodrow Wilson. Wilson, who was more favorable to government control than to banker control, called the new Congress into special session in the spring of 1913; various compromises were hammered out just before Christmas. Many politicians were afraid of giving too much power to Wall Street bankers, while others feared giving excessive power to the federal government in Washington.

But both groups felt there was a need for a more "elastic" currency, which could expand when the public demanded it, thereby preventing the contraction of bank credit as happened under the then-current system. Carter Glass, the Democrat who sponsored the bill in the House of Representatives, changed the name to the Federal Reserve System, but otherwise presented a bill quite similar to the Aldrich Bill. Senator Robert Owen was the sponsor in the Senate. A main difference was that the president, and not the large bankers, would appoint members of the Federal Reserve Board in Washington. Another difference was that this act allowed all of the twelve Federal Reserve Banks to set their own discount rates, but the act itself set the reserve ratios for deposits rather than leave this up to the central bankers. The Aldrich Bill would have had one discount rate among its fifteen branches.

The 1913 act provided for a Federal Reserve Board in Washington with five governors appointed by the President and confirmed by the Senate, plus two *ex-officio* members, the Secretary of the Treasury and the Comptroller of the Currency. One of the initial appointees to the Federal Reserve Board was Paul Warburg, perhaps a signal to the Republicans that President Wilson was not overly influenced by the populist wing of his party and wanted some connection with New York banking interests.

To avoid the appearance of one central monetary authority, twelve regional Federal Reserve Banks were established around the country in Boston, New York, Philadelphia, Richmond, Cleveland, Chicago, Atlanta, St. Louis, Kansas City, Minneapolis, Dallas and San Francisco. These district Federal Reserve Banks were to be owned by the member banks in their district, with each bank buying stock in the Federal Reserve Bank equal to 3 percent of its capital and surplus. Each member bank received a 6 percent dividend on this stock. Each of the twelve Federal Reserve Banks was supervised by a board of nine directors, six of whom were elected by the member banks while the other three were appointed by the Federal Reserve Board in Washington. The nine directors elected the head official at the district Federal Reserve Bank; he was then called a governor.

The purpose of the Federal Reserve Act was to "provide an elastic currency" and a means to discount commercial paper, and a better method of check collection and bank supervision. The new federal reserve note was to be that new currency, which member banks could borrow by re-discounting commercial paper, a short-term loan banks made to firms to finance the production and sale of goods. Member banks were to hold their reserve deposits at their district Federal Reserve Bank, and not in private banks in the money centers as before. It was thought that each district Federal Reserve Bank would have its own discount rate that it charged for the loans to member banks. In order to convince the public that the Federal Reserve System was not going to violate the gold standard, each district Federal Reserve Bank had to hold gold equal to 40 percent of its federal reserve notes issued, and 35 percent of the reserve deposits of member banks.

The gold standard required nations to follow automatic rules wherein the money supply would expand when gold flowed into a nation, and contract when gold flowed out. No discretion was permitted. Prices would rise with gold inflows and fall with gold outflows or when the supply of goods rose faster than the money supply. But the Federal Reserve used discretion by following the now discredited "real bills doctrine," which was supposed to expand the money supply when the needs of trade demanded it, as evidenced by commercial banks wanting to re-discount commercial paper at the Federal Reserve for more currency or an addition to their reserve account there. This real bills doctrine, believed more by bankers than academic economists, argued that if banks restricted their lending to short-term liquid loans for real production, then the needs of trade would regulate the supply of money, preventing inflation or deflation. Other economists pointed out that the total supply of money and bank credit cannot be controlled by restricting its first use. Furthermore, if the market for commercial paper were to dry up, these loans would not be self-liquidating without a central bank willing to buy them with newly injected money.

A conflict could arise if American citizens wanted to buy more foreign goods or invest more in foreign nations than foreigners wanted to buy or invest here. That would call for an outflow of gold, and hence, a shrinking of the money supply. But simultaneously banks could be making a lot of commercial loans and would want to re-discount them at the Federal Reserve, which would cause the money supply to rise. The Fed would be torn between lowering the discount rate to encourage member bank borrowing, and raising that rate to discourage purchases from abroad and American investment overseas. The higher discount rate would possibly attract foreign gold to the U.S., which would expand the domestic money supply. In any case, the Fed would be using discretionary policy rather than following the gold standard's automatic rules.

2

The Aldrich-Vreeland Act
Prevents a Panic in 1914

The Federal Reserve Act was passed in December 1913, but the twelve Federal Reserve Banks did not begin operation until November 1914. Therefore, this law extended the provisions of the Aldrich Vreeland Act, which allowed national banks to form national currency associations for one year to June 30, 1915. Originally, the permission to issue emergency currency was to expire at the end of June 1914. The Federal Reserve Act also reduced the tax on this emergency currency to 3 percent annually for the first three months, after which the tax was to rise half a point each month until a maximum of 6 percent was reached. Some other restrictions on issuance were also lifted. Banks no longer had to have regular bank notes outstanding equal to 40 percent of their capital and surplus before they could issue emergency currency. Moreover, the Aldrich Vreeland Act was amended to permit banks to issue the new currency up to 125 percent, rather than 100 percent of their capital and surplus. Congress also repealed the provision that limited the total issuance to $500 million.

The extension and modification of the Aldrich Vreeland Act proved to be a fortunate move. When World War I broke out in Europe in August 1914, England demanded payment of all loans in gold and set up a special depository in Ottawa, Canada to receive shipment. This caused another liquidity crisis because the reserves of the New York banks were depleted by the large exports of gold. In addition, the public demanded more currency while the New York stock exchange closed from July 31 to December 12. The national bank notes that were issued under this law prevented the suspensions of cash payments by banks as had occurred in the panics of 1873, 1893 and 1907. A total of $386.4 million was issued, or about a one-seventh increase in total currency outstanding, which allowed banks to satisfy the public's demand for currency by exchanging one liability for another (bank notes for deposits) without using their reserves of gold or greenbacks. Once the public and the small country banks found out they could get currency, they stopped demanding it. Some of these emergency national bank notes were returned to the Bureau of Engraving unopened in their original packages.

Without the use of this emergency currency, it is highly probable that the U.S. banking system would have had to suspend cash payments as it had done in 1907. By mid–October, which was 10 weeks after the crisis began, over $368 million of new bank notes were outstanding, But on August 1, national banks owned only about $12 million of government bonds that were eligible for backing regular national bank notes. A total of $137.5 million of these eligible bonds were outstanding but not owned by national banks. This meant that a maximum of only $149.5 million of new bank notes could have been issued if the national banks could have purchased these bonds quickly. That amount is less than half the amount of emergency currency issued by mid–October.

By January 1915, 60 percent of the emergency issue had been retired, while the balance was retired by June, except for $200,000 issued by a bank in Pennsylvania that failed. The new federal reserve note played very little role in this crisis, which caused some academic economists to question the need for the Federal Reserve. This emergency currency expanded quickly when needed and contracted just as fast, probably to avoid paying any additional tax on it. During the first week of August, $100 million was issued, and another $56.1 million was put in circulation the following week. Those were the largest amounts put out in any week. The public accepted the new money completely because it was indistinguishable from regular bank notes. The only minor problem was the fact that bankers had too many $50 and $100 bills and not enough small denominations. By mid–August the Bureau of Engraving was working day and night to print small bills, because the large ones were not in demand.

In 1914, some clearinghouses still issued clearinghouse loan certificates but the rate of interest on such loans was 6 percent, compared to the 3 percent tax on the new emergency currency. State banks, even those who had joined the Federal Reserve System, were not eligible to issue emergency bank notes, nor were trust companies. Only 12 clearinghouses issued these certificates in 1914, compared to 51 in 1907. The actual amount issued in 1914 was very close to the amount used in 1907, but in 1914 it was only 1.47 percent of total deposits, compared to 2.57 percent in 1907. The new emergency currency made it unnecessary to issue clearinghouse loan certificates in small denominations to use as hand-to-hand currency, as in the previous crisis. As further proof of the confidence the new currency gave the public, the Comptroller of the Currency and the New York Superintendent of Banks publicly asked for reports on the usage of these loan certificates in 1914. In contrast, their use had been kept secret in 1907 to prevent further panic. These loan certificates remained outstanding for only 118 days in 1914, compared to 154 days in 1907 and 133 days in 1893. The new emergency currency provided cheaper liquidity to banks. In New York City alone, less than $50 million of clearinghouse loan certificates remained outstanding during the first week of October 1914, after $100 million had been issued in August.

The tax on the emergency bank notes was an incentive for banks to withdraw them as soon as they were not needed. Deposits came quickly back to the bank on which they are drawn through clearinghouse settlements. In contrast, the regular national bank notes remained in circulation for some time because they were uniform, and banks often paid out each other's notes, or state-chartered banks used them for reserves. But in Canada, each bank issued its own distinctive bank notes, which were returned quickly to the issuer because each bank was eager to gets its own notes out and to drive its rivals' notes out of circulation. The U.S. national bank notes lacked such a market force to control their circulation, so the tax on this emergency currency was the incentive for redemption.

One probable reason why the twelve Federal Reserve Banks played an insignificant role in this crisis involved cost. The Federal Reserve began operations on November 16, 1914, with a discount rate of 5½ percent at the New York Fed. By this time, the tax rate on the emergency currency had risen to only 3½ percent. During this particular week in November 1914, the amount of emergency currency outstanding was $322.6 million, while the new federal reserve note was issued at a very slow rate. Only $1.2 million was put into circulation the first week, and only $17.2 million was outstanding by January 2, 1915. The impact of Christmas shopping could have influenced some of this issue.

In fact, the federal reserve note was never able to replace national bank notes until the latter were forcibly removed from circulation by the Banking Act of 1935. The Fed was authorized to purchase from the national banks the 2 percent bonds that backed these bank notes in the 1920s. But because short-term interest rates fell, these bonds rose above par and the Fed refused to pay more than face value for them. As a result, $727 million of national bank notes were still circulating in 1933, which exceeded the amount that were in existence before the Fed began operations in 1914.

Even though the American banking system was still hampered by lack of nationwide branching and still required the use of fixed cash reserves or deposits in money center banks as reserves, the mere permission of banks to convert deposit liabilities into bank note liabilities prevented the suspension of cash payments and widespread panic in 1914. The required currency increase was only about 11 percent over twelve weeks. The total currency of all forms outside the Treasury on August 1, 1914, was $3.4 billion. The maximum amount of emergency currency outstanding at any time was $368.6 million on October 24. This was a strong indication that there was no need for a Federal Reserve to increase the money base, as it would do when it extended credit to the banking system. Some American economists of that period clearly recognized that the banking system could be fixed by branching and an easier method of issuing bank notes when demanded, but the politicians representing areas in which the small banks operated wanted to preserve the unit bank system.

3

Original Uncertainty Regarding Exercise of Fed Authority

Since the Federal Reserve Act was a compromise between those who wanted a central monetary authority and those who strongly opposed it, the act did not specify what would happen if there was a conflict between the Federal Reserve Board in Washington and any of the twelve district banks. Each district bank was allowed to set its own discount rate and each could buy government bonds to earn interest, which it needed to pay expenses including the 6 percent dividend on its stock. The governor of each of these twelve banks, had a higher salary than the board members in Washington.

The first leader (then called governor) of the Federal Reserve board, was Charles Hamlin, appointed by President Wilson. But since the Secretary of the Treasury and the Comptroller of the Currency were *ex-officio* members of the Board, the Fed had difficulty establishing its independence. The Secretary of the Treasury presided over all the meetings, and since the Secretary of the Treasury, William McAdoo, was President Wilson's son-in-law, it was difficult for Hamlin to take charge. In addition, Hamlin had been Assistant Secretary of the Treasury under McAdoo before he was appointed to the board. Unlike today, the Fed did not have its own building in Washington, but met in the Treasury Department's building.

The terms of the five members of the Federal Reserve Board were staggered. Hamlin's term was the shortest: just two years. His tenure as governor was marked by disputes not only with the Treasury Department over ruling authority, but also with the governors of the twelve district Federal Reserve Banks. Hamlin was reappointed to a ten-year term as a member of the Board in 1916 by President Wilson and reappointed to another ten year term by president Coolidge in 1926. But he was not a strong, dynamic leader. He viewed his job of governor as being the leader of a discussion group. He did not want to make even minor decisions without the board's approval. Hamlin also set up a large number of committees to cover various aspects of monetary matters. But since there were only five members on the Board, each member had to serve on several committees. This produced redundance when each matter had to be discussed first in committee and then before the full board — which consisted of practically the same people.

The other members of the original Federal Reserve Board were William P. G. Harding, an Alabama banker; Frederic A. Delano, president of the Chicago, Indianapolis and Louisville Railroad (and an uncle of Franklin D. Roosevelt); Adolph C. Miller, an academic economist from the University of California; and Paul Warburg, a New York investment banker and very strong advocate for a central bank for the United States.

Four of the five members of the board were approved without a Congressional hearing, but Warburg was subjected to one. At first he refused because he believed he was being unfairly singled out because of either his Wall Street connections or his German ancestry. Warburg was a naturalized American citizen, but there were anti–German feelings after the war in Europe began in August 1914. President Wilson persuaded Warburg to relent and he did. But when his term expired in 1918, Warburg stepped down because there were some in Congress who did not want someone on the Federal Reserve Board whose brothers were prominent figures in the German banking industry.

One controversy arose shortly after the Fed began operations. In 1915 Adolph Miller, with the support of board members Harding, Warburg and Delano, wanted to reduce the number of district Federal Reserve Banks from twelve to eight. (The law provided for not less than eight nor more than twelve banks). The district Federal Reserve Banks that this group wanted to eliminate were in Dallas, Minneapolis, Atlanta and Kansas City. Miller wanted larger district banks so each would have enough capital to carry on its operations. But Governor Hamlin, who acquiesced in Secretary McAdoo's leadership of the board, objected to the subject being discussed when the secretary was out with an illness. Before the next meeting, Hamlin, with Mr. McAdoo's insistence, got the legal opinion of Attorney General Thomas Gregory that the board had no power to reduce the number of district Banks. In April 1916, Gregory also ruled that the board had no power to move any district bank to another city.

Another problem during Hamlin's short tenure as governor was the establishment of the Council of Governors, an extralegal group of bankers and financiers representing the large banks. This group acted as if they were running monetary matters and the Federal Reserve Board was there only to ratify their decisions. The council, chaired by the governor of the New York Federal Reserve Bank, was to evolve into a very important decision-making body after the war in Europe ended. Hamlin was mildly opposed to the existence of this council because it was usurping powers the board was supposed to have, but he took no strong action against it. The next governor, William P. G. Harding, did oppose it but he had to concentrate on the financing of World War I after April 1917. By the time the war was over, the New York Fed had assumed a leading role in monetary affairs under its governor, Benjamin Strong.

Another job that the Federal Reserve had to undertake was to set up a system of nationwide check clearing at par. This meant that banks could no longer charge writers of checks a fee for collection, a service which many banks used as a source of income. But membership in the Federal Reserve System was mandatory only for national banks, and even those banks could decline to become members by switching to a state charter. So the early years of the Fed were marked by attempts to entice banks to join the system.

The office of the Comptroller of the Currency was established during the Civil War when the National Bank System was started. The comptroller's office examined national banks. When the Federal Reserve began fifty years later, the comptroller, who was an *ex-officio* member of the Federal Reserve Board, refused to allow the Fed to examine national banks. This left the Fed to examine only those state banks that chose to join the system. The main attraction of membership was the privilege of borrowing from the Fed by discounting commercial paper. The Fed also collected checks and delivered currency without charge. But the disadvantage, especially to small banks, was the reserve requirement that, after 1917, could only be met by keeping a reserve (checking) account at the district Federal Reserve Bank. Small banks also had to use larger correspondent banks for services that the Fed did not supply. By keeping an account in a large correspondent bank, the small bank could use that as a reserve account and get cash delivery, loan participation, foreign exchange, and purchase and safe keeping of securities. If the small bank joined the Federal Reserve, it would be forced to hold another set of reserves, and the Fed did not pay interest on this deposit as the correspondent could do at that time. The Fed made several attempts to get more banks to join the system, by lowering reserve requirements and breaking down bank deposits into demand and time deposits. The latter were given a very low reserve requirement of 3 percent. Prior to this, there was no distinction between time and demand deposits. But the Fed could not get control of all the banks in the nation until the Banking Act of 1980.

4

The Federal Reserve's Role in World War I

The war in Europe began in August 1914, and the Fed did not begin operation until November 1914. As mentioned before, a panic was averted by the use of emergency national banknotes as authorized by the Aldrich Vreeland Act. But after this initial period of uncertainty, the U.S. experienced a boom financed by an influx of gold from Europe. This is how those countries paid for war materiel. The new gold inflow, which amounted to about $1.3 billion, was the basis for an increase in the money supply of about 43 percent, which caused prices to rise sharply. But prices did not fall in Europe as the assumptions of the gold standard would have predicted. Instead, those nations stopped converting their currencies into gold and issued fiat money, which was paper money not backed by gold but only by the government's decree. So the gold standard was not working the way it had before the war. The Federal Reserve Banks were not able to stem the rising prices because they did not then have the portfolio of securities they now have to sell on the open market. The money supply doubled between 1914 and 1920, while the price level rose over 90 percent.

The second governor of the Federal Reserve Board was William P. G. Harding, the Alabama banker appointed by President Wilson in order to give the board geographical diversity. Harding found out that while the country was at war, the Treasury would be running the show. The Fed could not be independent as the Act of 1913 intended it to be. But under Governor Harding, the Fed did become the Treasury's fiscal agent. Before the U.S. entered the war, the Treasury kept its funds either in commercial banks, where it could earn interest, or in its various sub-treasuries. But during the war the Treasury began to use the New York Federal Reserve Bank as its fiscal agent. The Treasury deposited its funds there, and the Fed collected and paid out these funds for the Treasury. The New York Fed also held the gold reserves of the Treasury, and helped it issue and retire securities. By 1920, the Independent Treasury System was abolished and the Federal Reserve had become the Treasury's fiscal agent.

The Treasury, first under William McAdoo and later under Carter Glass, insisted that the federal government should be able to sell its bonds at a low enough interest rate to make it easy to finance the war. Some of these bonds or short-term bills were sold to commercial banks that were allowed to borrow from the Fed to finance these purchases. Corporations and the general public were also encouraged to buy government bonds, and the banking system frequently financed these purchases. After an amendment to the Federal Reserve Act, banks were able to borrow from the Fed with government securities as collateral at a lower rate than on commercial paper and at a lower rate than the yield on the government bonds, making this profitable for the banks. This amendment obviously violated the original purpose of the Fed, which was to discount commercial paper for banks needing liquidity, but it would be unpatriotic to oppose the amendment. The Fed did not buy the government bonds itself, as it would later do in World War II, but made the funds available for commercial banks and the general public to buy them.

One member of the Federal Reserve Board, Adolph C. Miller, was opposed to the Treasury borrowing from the public at interest rates that were below market rates. Miller was the lone economist on the board and argued that the government should reduce consumption by the public in order to reallocate resources to the government to fight the war. This would largely entail higher taxes, but Miller felt that this would be better than allowing too much spending power to lead to inflation. If inflation were to occur, Miller then stated that reliance on tight money and high interest rates could choke off needed private investment. Miller also believed that the Treasury's attempt to persuade the public to curtail private spending by appealing to patriotism would be ineffective.

The Federal Reserve under Governor Harding could not prevent inflationary spending because banks could get new reserves (lending power) by borrowing them from the Fed on government securities and then lending for any purpose. About six months after the war ended, a large increase in spending caused prices to rise through the end of 1919. The district Federal Reserve Banks kept their discount rates low to help the Treasury finance its Victory Loan Bond drive in the spring of 1919. Afterwards, they felt obligated to the Treasury to keep the cost of borrowing low. If the Fed refused to lend to commercial banks on these government securities, their prices would fall in the market, and hence the yields on them would rise. Governor Harding believed that if the newly created Fed did not cooperate with the established Treasury, it could be reduced to a department of the Treasury, or even abolished.

The Treasury finally did give the Fed permission to raise its discount rate at the end of 1919, and almost immediately the country went into a sharp economic depression. This downturn, while deep, was relatively short. Prices and output fell, and unemployment rose. Even after the depression was under way, the Fed raised the discount rate to 7 percent in June 1920 and kept it high for about a year. Thus, the Fed's action made the expansion worse in 1919, and the depression worse in 1920 and early 1921. Unemployment rose to over 11 percent in 1921, and the price level fell almost 19 percent between 1920 and 1922. Farm prices fell the most; American agriculture suffered hard times that would last until World War II. Congress soon thereafter added a sixth appointed member of the Federal Reserve Board who would represent agriculture.

The real leader of the Federal Reserve was located not in Washington, D.C., but in New York. He was Benjamin Strong, the governor of the New York Federal Reserve Bank. All twelve district Federal Reserve Banks were supposed to be equal, but the New York Fed was and still is "more equal" than the others. It is situated where the money market is, and Benjamin Strong was very much an activist. After the experience of the 1920–1921 depression, he stopped subscribing to the real bills doctrine, wherein the Fed would passively accommodate commercial banks' demand for new reserves when the volume of trade increased. Strong wanted the Fed to buy and sell bankers' acceptances and government bonds to change the amount of bank credit in the system. Bankers' acceptances are financial instruments used to fund foreign trade. They became important money market instruments after World War I, when the New York became the leading money center of the world.

But Strong was also a firm believer in the gold standard. When the war was over in November 1918, the government changed its policy of forbidding the export of gold. Gold did flow out of the United States in 1919 and 1920. Strong, along with Treasury officials, firmly believed that the Federal Reserve must maintain a 40 percent backing for its federal reserve notes and a 35 percent backing for commercial bank reserve deposits. This meant that the Federal Reserve's discount rate had to remain high, even though the economy was in a depression. It was Strong who sacrificed domestic stability to the international gold standard, but it was William P. G. Harding who suffered the consequences. The sharp downturn in the economy and high unemployment were blamed on the Federal Reserve Board. When Harding's term was up in 1922, he was not reappointed. A new president, Warren G. Harding (no relation to William), wanted to appoint his boyhood pal, Daniel Richard "Dick" Crissinger, as Governor of the Federal Reserve Board. William P. G. Harding moved to the position of Governor of the Boston Federal Reserve Bank at twice his old salary. Crissinger took over a job for which he was not qualified, even though he had been an *ex officio* member of the board since mid–1921 when President Warren G. Harding had made him Comptroller of the Currency. This meant that the real power of the Federal Reserve was to rest even more with the New York Fed and Benjamin Strong.

The entry of the United States into the war, as previously mentioned, was the impetus for the Treasury to make the Federal Reserve Bank of New York its sole fiscal agent. Both McAdoo and Strong pushed hard for this change. The Independent Treasury System, which could trace its history back to the time of Andrew Jackson, was terminated in 1920. This permitted the New York Fed to sell and distribute nearly half of all the bonds the Treasury offered during the war. The New York Fed also handled the Treasury's foreign exchange business and became the main depository of other Reserve Banks and of foreign banks in the United States.

Benjamin Strong was able to have the New York Fed acquire most of the nation's gold stock as a result of the war. In 1917, after the U.S. entry into the conflict, Congress changed the law to allow the issuance of federal reserve notes in exchange for gold (instead of commercial paper as the act had originally stated). Congress also changed the rule regarding where member banks could hold their required reserves. After 1917, all bank reserves had to be held on deposit at their respective district Federal Reserve Banks, which eliminated vault cash as a legal reserve even though commercial banks still had to have this cash to operate. This was a hardship for banks located at some distance from their district Federal Reserve Banks, because they had to hold more vault cash than did those that were close enough to get speedy deliveries of federal reserve notes. As a result of the New York Fed's influence, its particular gold holdings rose from $720 million, which was 28 percent of the nation's monetary gold, to $2.1 billion in 1918, or 74 percent of the total.

5

The Discovery of a New Tool for the Federal Reserve

The Federal Reserve Banks were given the power to buy government bonds to earn the income they needed to pay dividends on their outstanding stock and the salaries of their employees. Another reason for the bond purchases was to back an emergency currency used during the war. This currency was called "Federal Reserve Bank Notes," which, unlike regular federal reserve notes, did not have any gold *backing*. Instead, they had the same backing the national bank notes had (government bonds) and were issued on the same type of paper, labeled *National Currency*. In 1918, these Federal Reserve Bank Notes were issued under provisions of the Pittman Act to retire $350 million in silver certificates. The silver certificates were withdrawn when the silver dollars were melted down and this bullion was sold to Great Britain, which needed the silver to make purchases from India. This same emergency currency was retired after the war by reissuing new silver certificates, after the government bought additional silver in the domestic market. These Federal Reserve Bank Notes were later issued in the Depression of the early 1930s and again during World War II.

But the twelve district Federal Reserve Banks were originally acting individually in their bond purchases. These banks soon discovered that after making bond purchases, the commercial banks not only reduced their borrowing via the discount mechanism but also repaid their indebtedness. On the other hand, when the Fed sold government bonds, the commercial banks had to borrow more extensively from their respective Federal Reserve Banks, and also tended to curtail their lending to firms. It then became apparent that the Fed had a tool with which it could actively change commercial bank reserves and lending power, without passively waiting for these banks to come to the Fed and borrow reserves.

This new tool, called "open market operations," is the main tool the Fed currently uses to conduct monetary policy. But in the early 1920s, the twelve district banks did not have to participate as a unit as they do now. The difference between these two approaches to monetary policy can be seen in the following illustration:

Discounting Commercial Paper

Commercial Bank		Federal Reserve Bank	
Assets	Liabilities	Assets	Liabilities
-Com Pap		+ Discounts	+ Reserves
+ Reserves			or + Fed Res Notes
or +Fed Res Notes			

With discounting, the initiative is with the member bank; the Fed passively accommodates the need for new federal reserve notes or an increase in the bank's reserve account at the Fed.

With open market operations, the Fed initiates the action by purchasing bonds (or bankers' acceptances) on the open market:

Commercial Bank		Federal Reserve Bank	
Assets	Liabilities	Assets	Liabilities
+Res	+ Deposits	+ Bonds	+Res

The above illustration assumes that a customer of the commercial bank, such as a bond trader, sold the bonds to the Fed and deposited the Fed's check in the bank. If the bank itself sold the bonds to the Fed, it would trade one asset for another — bonds for reserves — but all these reserves would be available for supporting new loans. This is an addition to total reserves, which is the case whenever the Fed buys securities or makes a loan. On the other hand, when a check is written on one commercial bank and deposited in another, no new reserves are created because the second bank gains what the first one loses.

The Federal Reserve board under its new governor, Dick Crissinger was often in conflict with both Secretary of the Treasury Andrew Mellon and the governor of the New York Federal Reserve Bank, Benjamin Strong. Before Crissinger was appointed governor of the board, President Harding had appointed him Comptroller of the Currency. Thus both he and Mellon were *ex-officio* members of the board in Washington, where the two often disagreed on policy. Mellon tried to talk the President out of appointing Crissinger as governor of the board. However, Harding wanted his old friend in that position not only because of their friendship, but also because of Crissinger's desire for low interest rates, which represented the wishes of the agricultural sector as opposed to the more restrictive policies of Mellon and Strong.

The Treasury was concerned with the lack of cooperation among the district Federal Reserve Banks in conducting open market operations. So in the spring of 1922 the Fed, at the encouragement of Andrew Mellon and Benjamin Strong, set up the Committee of Governors on Centralized Execution of Purchases and Sales of Government Securities by Federal Reserve Banks. This committee was dominated by Benjamin Strong, not only because of the force of his personality but also because the money market was located in New York. But when Strong had to take a leave of absence for health reasons, the Federal Reserve Board, at the encouragement of Adolph Miller and Secretary of Commerce Herbert Hoover, abolished this committee in March 1923. It then set up the Open Market Investment Committee, under the jurisdiction of the board, even though the same persons were on both of the committees. While Strong was opposed to this change, he actually retained as much or more influence because the new arrangement reduced the influence of the other district banks' governors.

The Open Market Investment Committee was set up with five district bank governors and the board in Washington to oversee purchases and sales of government securities. Benjamin Strong was chairman of this committee. The idea was to have the twelve banks act in unison, with each taking a pro-rata share of the transactions. However, any district bank could opt out if it wished (unlike today). Since the money market was located in New York, that district bank achieved a position of dominance in making Fed policy. With Benjamin Strong having Secretary Mellon on his side most of the time, conflicts with Crissinger and Miller at the board in Washington were usually resolved in favor of the New York Fed and the Treasury.

The federal government's debt increased because of the war. Now the Fed had plenty of securities to buy if it wanted to expand the money supply, and lower interest rates to make it easier for foreigners to borrow in the New York money or capital market. Benjamin Strong reconvened a conference of governors on a regular basis in order to encourage the twelve district Federal Reserve Banks to cooperate in open market operations. But when Strong was out ill from February to October 1923, Adolph Miller tried to wrest control from Strong and the New York Fed by establishing more board control over the Open Market Investment Committee. However, when Strong returned in October, he was able to gain control of that committee and keep control until his death in October 1928. He created a Special System Investment Account at the New York Fed in which all committee bond purchases were kept. This change reduced the influence of the other district banks, and so made Strong a more important figure. He also announced he would use open market purchases to lower interest rates to encourage investment if the economy were to slow down. In other words, he was willing to use the new tool actively to prevent economic downturns, and not merely rely on member banks to initiate the borrowing by sending commercial paper to the their district Federal Reserve Bank.

Strong was concerned with the international gold standard, and particularly with Great Britain's attempt to return to the prewar gold parity. He wanted to cooperate with the Bank of England in its effort to return to the old system. Therefore, he wanted an easy money policy with low interest rates, which would prevent the U.S. from gaining new gold and would thereby, help gold flow to Britain. Strong wanted to reduce the power of the board; he encouraged district banks to purchase securities for their own accounts when the discount rate was increased. Adolph Miller and his friend Herbert Hoover, Secretary of Commerce under presidents Harding and Coolidge, wanted more power in the board. Miller and Hoover feared that an easy money, low interest rate policy would fuel stock market speculation. They were much less interested in cooperation with foreign central banks. Instead, they believed the Fed should be concerned primarily with domestic price stability.

6

The Fed in the 1920s

Although the 1920s were generally a prosperous period, the Fed did have some problems in that decade. Agriculture was depressed soon after World War I was over. Prices of farm products fell, and between 5,000 and 6,000 banks failed, mostly in rural areas. While some of these banks were nationally chartered, hence members of the Federal Reserve system, most were state-chartered or even privately run banks with no charter, and thus not members of the Fed. This meant that the Federal Reserve was not immediately concerned with the fate of these small banks, but they should have been. Non-member banks keep reserve accounts in member banks, and when these reserves are withdrawn, the member banks feel pressure to contract their lending. Benjamin Strong at the New York Fed wanted to make membership in the Federal Reserve system compulsory for all state banks as a way to centralize gold reserves. When the Depression began after 1929, it became apparent that bank runs were contagious. Many more banks failed (9,000 between 1929 and 1933) while the public lost all confidence in the American banking system.

The framers of the Federal Reserve Act believed that if commercial banks restricted their lending to companies who were going to use it for productive purposes and not speculation, the problems of inflation and deflation would be avoided. This theory, now discredited, was called the "real bills doctrine" or "commercial loan theory." The thinking behind it was that the supply of money should expand and contract with the "needs of trade." Carter Glass, the main sponsor of the

41

Federal Reserve Act in the House of Representatives, was convinced that the real bills doctrine was the way to prevent inflation or deflation. Even the one economist on the original Federal Reserve board, Adolph C. Miller, was a believer in the real bills doctrine. This theory assumes that short-term loans made to finance goods in production would be self-liquidating, because the loan could be repaid from the profits of selling the goods. The money supply from bank lending would rise while the loan was outstanding, and contract when the loan was repaid. Obviously, the loan would not be self-liquidating if the goods were not sold.

But more importantly, it is not possible to control total expansion of the money supply by restricting its first use. Money is the most liquid of all assets and can be exchanged for any other good, including those of a speculative nature. But the idea of the commercial loan theory was embedded in the Federal Reserve Act, because it limited borrowing at the district banks to loans secured by short term commercial paper. This was to become a big problem once the Depression began. Benjamin Strong realized the fallacy of this doctrine; it was he who advocated the use of open market operations as the key tool for the Federal Reserve to regulate credit. Strong also wanted to set up a good secondary market for bills of exchange and bankers' acceptances, so that banks could use this as a source of liquidity rather than call loans to stockbrokers — loans that were based on speculative ventures.

Another problem faced by the Fed in the 1920s was the conflict between maintaining domestic stability and re-establishing the international gold standard. European nations had gone off gold during the war, and several were trying to restore that system in the 1920s. When U.S. business was expanding, there was a tendency for prices to rise. The Fed would then raise the discount rate and sell government securities to reduce bank reserves and lending power. But these higher interest rates would encourage foreigners to deposit gold in the U.S. The rules of the gold standard would require that prices rise in the U.S. and fall in countries losing gold. But the sale of government bonds by the Fed acted to sterilize the incoming gold, so prices here did not rise. Thus, there was no correcting mechanism for the gold flowing into the U.S.

Benjamin Strong believed that it was important to re-establish the gold standard. It was he, and not the board in Washington, who took the lead in meeting with the heads of the banks of England, France and Germany to achieve that end. In 1927, Strong met secretly in New York with Monagu Norman of the Bank of England; Charles Rist of the Bank of France; and Hjalmar Schacht of the German Reichsbank to push for a lower discount rate to keep more gold from flowing into the U.S. This meeting was kept secret even from the Federal Reserve Board in Washington. Many observers later felt that this move fueled banks' funding the excessive stock speculation prior to the 1929 crash. That was certainly the view of Adolph C. Miller, who was antagonistic toward Benjamin Strong, especially since the Federal Reserve Board was not apprised of this secret meeting. Banks used the excess lending power to purchase speculative securities. The lower rates also made it cheaper for brokerage firms and other non-bank lenders to finance stock market speculation. In fact, the high rates in the New York stock market attracted a good deal of loanable funds for speculation from many sources.

As a side issue, this low-interest policy led to a conflict between Federal Reserve Board Governor Crissinger and Benjamin Strong that ended with Crissinger resigning in November 1927. Paradoxically, both men were in favor of lower discount rates. Each district bank, except for the Chicago Fed, lowered its rate. When Crissinger tried to order the Chicago Fed to comply with lower rates, Strong opposed this because he felt the board was acting beyond its authority and violating the independence of each district bank. Even though Crissinger had the support of two of President Harding's Federal Reserve board appointees, George R. James and Edward H. Cunningham, he was opposed by the dominant figure in the Federal Reserve System. The dispute got nasty, but with Mellon and Strong against him, Crissinger resigned because he no longer had President Harding to support him.

President Coolidge replaced Crissinger with Roy Young, who had been governor at the Minneapolis Fed. His salary immediately dropped from $25,000 a year to $12,000, but he was now supposedly the top monetary official in the country. This was the only new Fed governor that President Coolidge was to appoint to the Federal Reserve board.

Coolidge did, however, reappoint Charles Hamlin, Adolph Miller, and Vice-governor Edmund Platt during his time in office. Roy Young believed that the gold standard should be maintained and that the Federal Reserve should accommodate commercial bank needs to finance business loans. Even though these two goals often conflicted, Young seemed able to convince himself there was no conflict. For the first year of Young's tenure, Benjamin Strong was the most powerful person in the Federal Reserve system, so Young reluctantly followed his lead. When the gold inflow was sterilized in 1927 by lowering the discount rate and buying bonds in the open market, Young believed this policy was the lesser of two evils. This policy kept interest rates low in the U.S., which discouraged foreigners from shipping more gold over here. But it also encouraged speculation in the stock market. With the discount rate low and interest on loans to brokers high, banks could profit by making these loans.

However, when Benjamin Strong died in October 1928, the Federal Reserve lost its real leader. He was replaced at the New York Fed by George Harrison, a man with whom Young often disagreed. Young also was frequently opposed by Vice-governor Edmund Platt, who was a tight money man and often had voted for higher discount rates. Platt, as a member of the House of Representatives in 1913, voted against the establishment of the Federal Reserve system. When the New York Fed wanted to raise its discount rate to curb speculation, Young disapproved because he felt that over-speculation would correct itself when speculators suffered losses.

One problem the Fed faced with the excessive stock speculation in 1928 and 1929 was that most of the loans on stocks came not from member banks, but from brokers and business firms. Banks could borrow from the Fed on legitimate commercial paper but then use those funds to lend to brokers at 12 percent in 1929. In addition, many firms no longer borrowed from banks to finance their output, but sold securities directly in the money and capital market, or used their retained earnings for that purpose. Banks, in order to counter the loss of commercial loans, set up affiliates to deal in securities and in the bonds of foreign nations. Young then argued for the Federal Reserve board to have the power to deny the discount privilege to any bank that used the funds for speculation. This was opposed by the New York Fed as an illegal interference in district Federal Reserve Bank operations. But such a power would not stop non-member banks from lending to brokers, nor non-banks from doing so. This disagreement on how monetary policy should be conducted had some very serious consequences when the economy plunged into the Great Depression.

President Coolidge apparently wanted a passive Federal Reserve board, and Roy Young seemed to agree with that philosophy. Young did not believe the Fed should try to influence the course of economic activity. Young believed the Fed should oversee the health of the banking system, which entailed issuing currency, rediscounting commercial paper, acting as a central clearinghouse for checks, and settling international payments. He did not feel that the Federal Reserve Act allowed the board to interfere in the economy. President Coolidge stated in January 1928 that the speculation in the stock market was not a cause for alarm, which reinforced Young's views that the Fed should not admonish banks about borrowing at the discount window and then lending these funds at higher rates in the New York call market. Since these call loans reached a high of 12 percent in 1929, while the discount rate at the New York District Bank did not rise to 6 percent until August of that year, there was a strong incentive to keep making these speculative loans.

What the Federal Reserve showed to observers in 1929 was a great deal of indecision and bickering among its officials. George Harrison, now governor at the New York Fed, was not able to convince Roy Young or enough board members of the need to raise the discount rate and engage in open market sales of securities while stock speculation was at its height. In addition, Charles Mitchell, president of the National City Bank of New York and a director of the New York Fed, defied the board by stating publicly that his bank was willing to lend $25 million to the call money market. These disagreements were to get worse and have much greater consequences for the economy after the stock market crash and the Depression got under way.

7

The Fed in the 1929–1933 Contraction

The October 1929 stock market crash did not cause the Great Depression. Rather, the crash reflected in part the fact that the economy had already turned down, and that the outlook was not bright. One of the most noticeable features of the U.S. financial system was its weak banking system that was to reach a point of desperation in early 1933. The Federal Reserve was created to prevent bank panics, but was now to preside over the worst series of bank failures in American history.

As noted earlier, before the Federal Reserve was established, bank panics were marked by banks suspending payment of currency, but not shutting down completely. Funds on deposit could still be transferred by check. Clearinghouses in major cities issued loan certificates to banks in distress, and these were often paid out in smaller denominations to the public for use as a currency substitute. The free market also worked to end the crisis. Currency commanded a premium over deposit money — as much as 4 percent in 1907. This premium drew currency out of hoards and as more currency emerged, the premium dropped and eventually disappeared. In the 1907 crisis, some Canadian bank notes circulated in the U.S. because Canadian banks did not face the restrictions on note issuance that the national banks did in this country. When the Aldrich Vreeland Act allowed national banks to issue an emergency currency in 1914, this prevented the need for banks to suspend currency payments or for clearinghouses to issue as many loan certificates as occurred in 1907. When the 1930s depression deepened and bank closings multiplied, some economists advocated the issuance of an emergency currency as had been done in 1914, but the Federal Reserve officials and Congress rejected this idea. They ignored the fact that, as pointed out earlier, small banks and the general public stopped demanding currency in 1914 when they found out they could get it.

After the stock market crash in late October 1929, the New York Fed lowered its discount rate and went into the open market to purchase $100 million of securities. This expansionary policy was the right thing to do. But when the Open Market Investment Committee recommended the purchase of another $200 million of bonds, George Harrison at the New York Fed could not convince Roy Young and other members of the board in Washington to agree to this. Eventually, this agreement was reached but with a delay that showed Fed indecision. This lack of consensus was soon to get worse. The Open Market Investment Committee (OMIC) was replaced in March 1930 by the Open Market Policy Conference (OMPC). The former, established in 1923, was composed of five reserve bank governors, with the New York governor acting as leader. However, decisions of the OMIC were subject to review by the board in Washington. When Benjamin Strong was at the New York Fed, the board often followed his lead, but George Harrison was not as persuasive a leader as Strong. The establishment of the Open Market Policy Conference further weakened the New York Fed's influence because it consisted of all twelve reserve Bank governors, some of whom resented New York's key role. This was further shown when Roy Young resigned from his position as governor of the board in August 1930 to become Governor of the Boston Federal Reserve Bank. In Boston, Roy Young had even more influence on open market policy as he consistently opposed Harrison's attempts to buy more securities.

Some Fed officials — Roy Young among them — felt the Federal Reserve Banks should protect their own reserve positions, which would allow them to lend to member banks later. Most economists would argue that a central bank should lend generously in a liquidity crisis and not worry about its own balance sheet. But Young's position asserted that even if the Fed did pump in more reserves to the banking system, most banks would hold the excess reserves and not use them to increase loans to business. In other words, Young felt that banks would hoard excess reserves and not use them to meet withdrawals or emergency loans to business.

In 1930, it was obvious that the bank runs were contagious. The public was losing faith in the banking system. This is quite different from the case of one particular bank being unsound and its depositors racing to withdraw funds to redeposit in another bank deemed to be safe. People were withdrawing their deposits in currency and hoarding this currency in safe deposit boxes or in cookie jars at home. When someone withdraws $100 in currency from a checking account, the bank loses $100 of vault cash and $100 of demand deposits, unless this happens to be a national bank that has some unissued bank notes in its vault. But the loss of vault cash to a state bank or any other type of currency to a national bank is a loss of $100 of reserves (base money), while the bank would be holding no more than $13 of reserves for that demand deposit and even less if it came from a time or savings account. Even though all member-bank-required reserves had to be held on deposit at their district Federal Reserve Bank, any vault cash still used up reserves dollar for dollar because the member bank had to pay for this vault cash by writing a check on its reserve account at the Fed. If a bank had no excess reserves when this withdrawal was made, it would have to sell some securities, or borrow from another bank or the Federal Reserve, to replenish these lost reserves. It becomes a chain reaction when all banks are faced with these runs on their vault cash. One bank can gain reserves by pulling its funds from a correspondent bank, but the system has no more reserves in the aggregate unless the Federal Reserve injects them by open market purchases of securities or lending to banks via the discount mechanism.

A bank that faced a run could borrow from its district Federal Reserve Bank if it had eligible commercial paper. But once the Depression started, there was a scarcity of commercial paper, which meant that the price of this financial instrument rose and therefore its yield fell. Even if the district Federal Reserve Bank lowered its discount rate, this rate might still be higher than the yield on commercial paper. Thus, a bank needing additional reserves to meet a run might find it more profitable to sell commercial paper in the open market to get the reserves it wanted, rather than borrow at the Fed. To a single bank, this was not important. But to the banking system it was crucial. When the Fed lent funds to a bank, this added new reserves to the system However, when a bank sold commercial paper in the open market, the amount of total reserves stayed the same (simply moving from one bank to another).

The weakness of the Fed was now apparent. With no dominant personality to take charge as Benjamin Strong had done in the 1920s, the Fed was now torn with discord. The Board was opposed to engaging in open market purchases, which could have pumped in enough money base to ease the panic. Adolph Miller was still on the board along with another original member, Charles S. Hamlin. Miller, whose friend Herbert Hoover was now in the White House, had been opposed to the New York Fed taking the lead either in open market operations or in changing the discount rate. Miller argued, somewhat strangely for an economist, that injecting new reserves into the system would cause banks to use them for speculative purposes, and that higher interest rates were needed to prevent an outflow of gold. Miller was also able to convince two other board members, George James and Edward Cunningham, to oppose purchases of government securities on the grounds that monetary policy was ineffective in combating business recessions. Charles Hamlin likewise believed the board should follow a passive, non-interventionist role.

When the Depression deepened, Adolph Miller finally realized that the Fed needed to take positive action to stem the downturn. But he was not able to persuade other members of the board to increase purchases of government securities. Miller even suggested the use of clearinghouse loan certificates as in the past, but no one followed his suggestion.

When Edward Cunningham died in November 1930, President Hoover replaced him in May 1931 with Wayland Magee, a director of the Kansas City Fed. But Magee's term expired in January 1933 and the Democratic Senate would not approve President Hoover's choice to reappoint Magee. So the board dropped to just four members during the most severe period of bank panic. The 1932 Glass-Steagall Act allowed any Federal Reserve bank, with the approval of five board members, to advance loans to a commercial bank on the latter's own note when such a bank did not have the normal collateral (commercial paper) to get a loan. But, with only four members, the board could not approve these needed loans.

Bank failures between October 1929 and March 1933 amounted to about 9,000, which reduced the number of banks in the nation to around 15,000 — half the number that had existed in 1921. These failures often occurred in waves while panic was at its worst. The first major wave occurred after October 1930, a year in which 1,350 banks failed. The most notable was the Bank of the United States, a private institution located in New York City, but with a name that could have led gullible depositors to think it was an official government institution. It was also a member of the Federal Reserve system with over $200 million in deposits. This was the largest bank failure in the country up until that time. Governor George Harrison of the New York Fed and the New York State Superintendent of Banks tried to convince the banks in the clearinghouse to save this bank, but they refused. Under the pre–Federal Reserve era, cash suspensions or loans from their clearinghouse might have saved this bank, but since the Fed existed, stronger banks in the clearinghouse association felt it was no longer their responsibility to help a bank in difficulty.

When Roy Young resigned as governor of the Federal Reserve board, President Hoover appointed Eugene Meyer to that position in September 1930. This was a recess appointment while Congress was not in session. Because Meyer had made millions as a Wall Street investor, the populist types in Congress opposed this move. His nomination was resubmitted in January 1931 and while his opponents ranted and raved about his Wall Street connections, they could not prevent his confirmation in late February. But by the time Meyer took his position, the conflicts between the board and the district banks were so intense that they prevented the Fed from stemming the contraction in bank deposits and the money supply. In March 1931, a second wave of bank failures began and was intensified by problems in Europe. In May,

Austria's largest bank, *Kreditanstalt,* failed which caused runs on other banks and some failures. This led banks to try to add to their reserves, and the public to withdraw more currency from banks. Some U.S. banks held short-term obligations of European banks which were now frozen assets. The only offset to this depressed condition was the inflow of gold, seeking a safer haven in this country.

Meyer felt George Harrison at the New York Fed was a weak leader. Harrison wanted the OMPC to authorize more bond purchases by the Fed but he waited until late June to make them because the OMPC met that month. Meyer thereafter decided to have the Federal Reserve Board meet with the OMPC before not after, they made their policy recommendations. But Meyer changed abruptly when Britain went off gold in September 1931.

When Britain declared it would no longer redeem its pound sterling in gold, there was a large increase in demand by Europeans for gold. Since the dollar was still redeemable in gold, there was a run on the dollar. Foreign central banks exchanged their dollar deposits at the New York Fed for gold. In six weeks, over $700 million of gold left the U.S. for Europe. Governor Meyer did believe that the gold standard should be maintained; therefore, he agreed with the New York Fed that it should raise its discount rate and stop open market purchases of securities. The belief in the gold standard was very strong among financial leaders in not only this country, but also in most European countries. But with central banks exercising discretion, the rules of the gold standard were often ignored, especially by the nation losing gold. This external pressure on banks from the loss of gold was matched by an internal drain by the public for more currency because people realized that many banks were failing. In 1931, a total of 2,293 banks failed. Banks losing reserves from the gold drain increased their borrowing from the Fed even though the discount rate was increased. Banks also dumped their commercial paper and government securities on the market to get needed reserves, but this caused the prices of these assets to fall and their yields to rise. By this dumping on the market, banks were only pulling reserves from one another.

The reason the Federal Reserve was so concerned by the drain of gold was that each district bank had to hold gold equal to 40 percent of its federal reserve notes and 35 percent of the reserves it was holding on deposit for member banks. In addition to gold backing, the federal reserve notes had to be backed by 60 percent eligible paper, but since commercial paper was scarce, the additional backing had to be in gold. This problem was partially alleviated by the passage of the Glass Steagall Act in February 1932. As mentioned before, this law allowed government bonds as well as commercial paper to serve as collateral for federal reserve notes, and further permitted member banks to borrow from the Fed on assets approved by the Federal Reserve board. Carter Glass himself was not enthusiastic about this bill, but he sponsored it hoping it would not be used. As one of the architects of the Federal Reserve Act in 1913, he believed in the real bills doctrine and did not want currency backed by government bonds. He considered this bill to be similar to those that wanted the government to print more greenbacks, which were pure fiat money not backed by anything. However, this law did little to stop the demand for currency by the public, which was causing the banking system to implode. The type of reform that would have helped, even if Carter Glass did not agree, would have been the use of the emergency currency that the national banks were authorized to issue under the Aldrich Vreeland Act, or giving the Federal Reserve Banks the power they had during the First World War to issue Federal Reserve Bank Notes, which were backed by government bonds and issued on the same paper as the national bank note. Neither the national bank notes nor the Federal Reserve Bank Notes required a gold backing.

Professor Allan Meltzer, in his recent study of the Fed, pointed out that the amount of U.S.-held gold was adequate for backing of federal reserve notes and reserve deposits, even with the outflow of gold that occurred after England left the gold standard. He points out that the Fed had $1 billion in gold reserve plus another billion in gold certificates, which could have replaced other types of currency. But the twelve Federal Reserve Banks acted independently and not as a unit during this crucial time.

Besides the decentralization of the Fed, another reason for the failure to expand open market operations to stem the contraction was the misguided belief in the real bills doctrine. This theory states that the central bank should provide credit to commercial banks to finance the needs of trade. With the business sector in depression, the theory would imply there was no need for credit expansion. Many Fed officials believed in this theory, so they felt it was up to commercial banks to come to the Fed to borrow reserves when they needed them. Supplying reserves through open market purchases of government securities would add redundant reserves that could be used for speculation. Many who held this belief, such as Governor Roy Young who moved to the board from the Minneapolis Fed, argued that the real bills doctrine had been violated in 1927 by Benjamin Strong when he lowered the discount rate and purchased bonds to help the Bank of England. In Young's view, this measure led to speculative excesses of 1928 and 1929, which needed to be corrected by contraction of credit and deflation. In addition, many governors of regional Federal Reserve Banks resented the New York Fed's position of dominance and were not eager to cooperate in open market purchases. Some governors even wanted the Fed to sell bonds to decrease bank reserves, which they hoped would force banks to borrow via the discount window.

Another unfortunate factor explaining Fed inaction was the mistaken belief that money and credit were already very easy because short-term interest rates were low. These rates were low compared to what they had been in times past, but in the deflation of the early 1930s, they were not low in real terms. If the price level was falling about 5 percent a year, then a 2 percent nominal rate would be 7 percent in real terms. In addition, George Harrison of the New York Fed stated in July 1930 that since most banks in New York had paid off their indebtedness to the Fed and were holding excess reserves, credit was easy and so there would be no need for open market purchases. In reality, these excess reserves were held for protection against bank runs by depositors and did not indicate monetary ease. By October 1930, real output had fallen about halfway from the peak of 1929 to what it would be at the trough in March 1933, but the price level had fallen to only about a quarter of the amount that it was to decline. This verified what many economists, such as Irving Fisher and John M. Keynes, had said: that output would feel the brunt of a decline in the money supply before the price level would.

Another attempt by the government to help stem the tide of bank failures was the passage of the Reconstruction Finance Corporation (RFC) in early 1932. Governor Eugene Meyer was largely responsible for writing this law, which was based on the War Finance Corporation of which Meyer had been a director in 1918. This new government agency was authorized to lend up to $2 billion to troubled financial institutions, but its effectiveness was severely limited by politics. Meyer was made chairman of the board of directors of the RFC, which put a strain on him (working mornings at the Fed and afternoons at the RFC). Originally, loans made by this agency to banks were not publicized in hopes of preventing the public from running on banks that were in need of assistance. But when the president of the RFC, Charles Dawes, resigned in July 1932 to operate his bank in Chicago and immediately received a loan from the RFC, the Democratic Speaker of the House, John N. Garner, demanded that all loans be made public to avoid favoritism. From that point on, the RFC was less effective because a loan from it signaled to depositors that their bank was in trouble, causing panicky runs.

Congress did put pressure on the Fed to expand its purchase of government bonds in the open market in the spring of 1932. The OMPC did purchase about $1 billion worth of securities by August of that year, but about half of this expansion in the money base was offset by the gold outflow of $500 million. Not all of the Federal Reserve Banks participated in these purchases. Roy Young, now of the Boston Fed, was opposed to this expansionary move. The New York Fed bought about 80 percent of the bonds, with the Cleveland, Philadelphia and Kansas City Feds the only others joining in.

In 1932, the country was in a desperate mood. There were pressures from some congressmen to pay the bonus to veterans of World War I right away, rather than wait until 1945, the year it was promised. In addition, other congressmen wanted to print greenbacks or Federal Reserve Bank Notes, like the ones that had been issued during the war. So the Glass Steagall Act, the Reconstruction Finance Corporation, and the open market purchases were all attempts to offset what many considered radical measures.

The reason for the Fed stopping these open market purchases in

August 1932 was either because member banks' discounts were very low, indicating credit was normal, or because the discounts did no good since bank lending did not increase. This was unfortunate because the money supply, defined as currency and demand deposits, increased as did industrial production between March and October 1932. Continued purchases, regardless of the impact on bank lending, may have helped stem the worst part of the contraction that occurred in early 1933.

By this time the public had lost all confidence in banks as a safe depository for their funds. The public kept increasing its demand for currency at the expense of deposits, and the banks reacted by increasing their demand for excess reserves. After Congress ended its session in August and the Fed stopped buying government bonds, there was a large contraction in the money base. Congress had passed a tax increase in 1932 in a vain attempt to balance the budget, an attempt which also hurt the depressed economy.

One small mitigating factor that helped satisfy some of the increased demand for currency after August 1932 was an increase in national bank notes of $140 million. Congress allowed them to be backed with government bonds that yielded up to 3¾ percent instead of the 2 percent that had been in effect since the Civil War. This measure was part of the Home Loan Bank Act of 1932. But the public's increase in the demand for currency at the expense of deposits far outstripped this increase in national bank notes.

Another example of the distrust of banks was the large increase in postal savings between 1929 and 1933. This program had been set up in 1910 for unsophisticated savers who were unlikely to deal with banks. Deposits in this system, which were absolutely safe, increased from $100 million in 1929 to $1.1 billion in 1933.

The increased demand for currency caused banks to increase their demand for excess reserves, which also caused a contraction of deposits. In order to get excess reserves, banks dumped their securities on the market, causing them to fall in price. This fall in the price of these securities, even the government's, hurt the banks that still had these bonds in their portfolio. Paradoxically, high-grade bonds could hurt a bank worse than lower-grade bonds for which no national market existed. Bank examiners marked down the high-grade bonds, such as federal government securities or private bonds traded and quoted on the bond market, that banks were holding because these had a current market value. If held to maturity, most of these bonds would be redeemed at face value. But if an obscure water district bond was not traded nationally, bank examiners would often list it at par value so long as the interest payments were current. If enough bank-held bonds were marked down, its capital could be impaired and the bank forced to close, even though it was merely illiquid and not insolvent.

Interestingly, life insurance companies did not face the same regulations regarding their bond holdings that banks did. The National Association of Insurance Administrators did not mark down bonds that insurance companies were holding if the bonds were not in default. Such a policy would have been beneficial to the banking industry.

The final bank panic was the worst, from January to March 1933, during a period when Herbert Hoover was still in office although he had been defeated in the November 1932 election by Franklin Roosevelt. (This was the last year that presidents were inaugurated in March and the last time we had a lame duck session of Congress.) The Fed by this time was paralyzed. There was no cooperation among the district banks and no direction from the board in Washington. This was evidenced by the failure of the Democratic senate to confirm the reappointment of Wayland Magee as a member of the Federal Reserve Board. Magee, as mentioned above, was originally appointed by President Hoover in May 1931 to fill the unexpired term of Edward Cunningham. Magee's term ended in January 1933 but the senate refused to act on Hoover's reappointment. This left only four members on the Federal Reserve board, which meant that the board could not approve advances to member banks on their promissory notes as authorized by the 1932 Glass Steagall Act, because that act required the approval of five board members. So if a bank did not have commercial paper, it could not borrow from its district federal bank at a crucial time.

The increase in the demand for currency now underwent a new phase. The public now demanded gold or gold certificates, and not federal reserve notes, greenbacks or national bank notes. There were fears, which turned out to be justified, that the Roosevelt administration would devalue the dollar. Governor Harrison at the New York Fed wanted to stop member banks from making safe deposit boxes available to those who wanted to hoard gold, and also wanted to prevent banks from making loans for gold speculation. However, he had no power to act. The Fed conducted no open market purchases during January or February 1933 but it did raise the discount rate, trying to protect gold from flowing out of the country. When the New York Federal Reserve Bank fell below its gold reserve requirements, the board suspended these requirements. Gold reserve requirements had also been suspended during World War I and would be suspended again during World War II.

Many states had declared bank holidays, wherein banks were closed. This was quite different from the 1907 panic when banks suspended currency payments but still stayed open to clear checks. In addition, a premium on currency in 1907 helped draw it out of hoards. None of this occurred in early 1933. The money stock, counting both currency and deposits, fell 12 percent in two months from January to March. Currency held by the public increased by $600 million but deposits fell by $2 billion, as banks also increased their reserve holdings by $65 million. This contraction of deposits was a result of their being fractionally backed, while currency in contrast used reserves dollar for dollar.

A nationwide bank holiday was declared on March 6, 1933, by President Roosevelt; it closed the banks that state governors had not already closed. When banks were allowed to open for business again, a total of 4,000 failed to reopen, making a total of 9,000 failures from 1929 to 1933. The money supply fell by a third during that four-year period, from $24 billion to $16 billion. Such a contraction of money was compounded by a decrease in the rate at which money was spent, called velocity. Velocity also fell by a third in that four-year period. When this happens, a severe deflationary pressure is exerted throughout the economy. This means that if prices are expected to fall, firms cannot produce at the current price level because they will not be able to cover their costs when the goods are sold at a lower price. Individuals postpone their purchases in expectation of further price decreases.

Deflationary expectations have not been experienced in this country since the 1930s, but their effect on the economy can be more devastating than inflationary expectations, which this nation experienced in the 1970s. When people expect prices to rise, they rush out to buy goods before prices go higher. Firms try to produce now and recover their profits by selling at higher prices. But inflationary expectations cannot carry an inflation very far unless the Fed pumps in more money. If the Fed tightens up, people may still expect prices to rise, but once they have spent their current income and borrowed all they can, they are unable to act upon these expectations. On the other hand, deflationary expectations do not have to be financed. The longer people wait to act, the smarter they seem to be. This would cause further price declines.

The prolonged depression of the 1930s had disastrous consequences for the entire nation. At its worst in 1933, over 25 percent of workers were unemployed, and many others had very low-paying jobs. This was before unemployment benefits were paid to workers who lost their jobs, so the hardship was far worse than today when workers lose their jobs. This prolonged depression did not have to happen. The Federal Reserve failed to keep the money supply from contracting when it had the tool (open market purchases of securities) to prevent it. Unfortunately, many Fed officials still believed in the discredited real bills doctrine. The public did not lose faith in banks until the fall of 1930, a year after the stock market crash. But once the public began withdrawing currency from the banking system and hoarding it, the multiplied contraction of deposits was difficult to stop. But as had been shown in 1914, once the public found out they could get the emergency currency authorized by the Aldrich Vreeland Act, they stopped demanding it and preferred to hold most of their funds in bank accounts.

As a significant contrast to the ordeal of American banking during this severe contraction period, it is enlightening to look at the Canadian banking experience. The Depression was just as severe in Canada as in the United States, with very high levels of unemployment. But the Canadian banks were able to go through this period with no bank failures, no central bank, and no deposit insurance. Unprofitable branches were closed but with no hardship to depositors. There were only eleven banks in Canada at the beginning of the downturn in 1929 and ten at the end of 1933 (because a small bank in Saskatchewan merged with a larger institution). Each bank was able to branch wherever it chose and could issue its own distinctive bank notes, which it always redeemed on demand for deposits or for base money (gold or Dominion Notes). The latter were issued in $1 and $2 bills by the government.

The reaction to the stock market crash in New York was quite different in the two nations, even though it was a severe deflationary shock in both. There was no increase in the demand to hoard base money (gold or Dominion Notes), or even bank notes in Canada. But in the United States, the public began to demand an increase in its currency holdings in October 1930, after the first big wave of bank failures started. Once this demand for currency got under way, it could only be satisfied by taking base money from a bank's vault cash — not by exchanging one liability for another, (deposits for bank notes) as Canadian banks could do. This is illustrated below:

Canadian Bank		U.S. Bank	
Assets	*Liabilities*	*Assets*	*Liabilities*
No change	+Banknotes	– Vault Cash	– Deposits
	–Deposits		

From October 1929 to October 1931, Canadian bank note liabilities fell 17 percent while deposits fell only 9 percent, indicating that the banks had plenty of unused note potential but the public was content to hold deposits. As the Depression deepened, the banks experienced a large decrease in borrowing by the business sector, so they increased their holdings of securities. In 1929, security holdings in Canadian banks were only 27 percent of loans but by late 1933, they had risen to 66 percent. Even with unemployment as high as in the United States, Canadian banks did not experience any currency runs (deposits to bank notes) or redemption runs (bank money to gold or Dominion Notes). The Canadians proved what the Americans proved with the Aldrich Vreeland emergency currency of 1914: once people realize that currency is readily available, they stop demanding it.

8

Policy Changes in the
Roosevelt Administration

When Roosevelt took office on March 4, 1933, many state governors had already declared bank holidays. FDR, using powers left over from World War I, declared a nationwide closing of all banks until Congress, which had been called into a special session, could enact emergency legislation. On March 9, an emergency act was passed that ordered the U.S. Treasury to acquire all outstanding gold and license all banks, and the Federal Reserve to issue more currency and make loans directly to businesses. Later that same year, the Thomas Amendment to the Agricultural Adjustment Act authorized the issuance of Federal Reserve Bank Notes, the emergency currency issued during the First World War that did not require any gold backing.

In May 1933, Eugene Meyer resigned as governor of the Federal Reserve board and was replaced by Eugene Black, who had been the governor at the Atlanta Fed. Black took this position on a temporary basis. He had met FDR at Warm Springs, Georgia, and was willing to help in a time of crisis. But his salary at the Atlanta Fed was twice his salary at the board. During Black's tenure, the closed banks were reopening as they received a license to do so; from none open on March 9, there were 14,016 open on August 30. Black was immediately concerned about the banks having enough lending power, so he was able to get the OMPC to engage in open market purchases of securities from May through November. However, when banks held on to a large amount of excess reserves, Black began speaking out that banks should lend more to businesses. Even though the Fed was authorized to lend directly to businesses, this did not occur because there were many restrictions put on this type of lending.

In August 1933, Congress passed the Banking Act of 1933, the Glass and Steagall Act, as the Banking Act of February 1932 had also (somewhat confusingly) been named. The 1933 act made some major changes in U.S. banking. Carter Glass had more enthusiasm for this bill than for the 1932 Act, which he hoped would not be used. The 1933 act forbad payment of interest by banks on their checking accounts (demand deposits) and limited to 3 percent the rate that could be paid on time deposits. Congress believed that this would prevent banks from excessive competition for deposits, which they believed would cause banks to make risky loans. However, this eased the pressure on banks to lend because their cost of deposits went down. In addition, this made it cheaper for the public to hoard currency because they could earn so little on deposits. This also meant that small banks could no longer earn interest on the balances they held in money center banks. Nonetheless, small banks were generally in favor of this prohibition because they believed that the large banks could afford to pay more interest on deposits, and hence draw funds away from the small banks.

The area where Carter Glass was most influential in the Banking Act of 1933 was the provision that separated deposit banking from investment banking. Glass was a believer in the real bills doctrine and blamed the speculative excesses of 1928 and 1929 on Benjamin Strong and his assistance to the Bank of England in 1927. Glass believed that by separating investment banking from commercial banking, the latter would not be able to finance speculative ventures and would concentrate on providing funds to businesses as the "needs of trade" arose. Glass also felt this measure would curb the power of the New York Fed.

The most important change that affected banking in 1933 was the provision in the Banking Act that called for federal insurance of bank deposits by a new agency, the Federal Deposit Insurance Corporation. This was primarily done at the insistence of Congressman Henry Steagall from Alabama, who had the interests of small country banks in mind. Carter Glass was not for deposit insurance but had to accept it as part of the bill. This was not a new idea. Many insurance proposals had been introduced into Congress since the Civil War, but all were rejected. When the Federal Reserve Act was passed in 1913, the Senate put in a deposit insurance plan but the House, led by then–Congressman Carter Glass, rejected it. Not only Glass but also FDR opposed it in 1933, but Henry Steagall pressed hard for it and Glass relented, because he believed coverage would be limited to member banks. The original law allowed non-member banks to apply for coverage because of the emergency, but required them to become members of the Fed by 1936. The small banks put enough pressure on their representatives in Congress to have that date moved back to 1942, but by then the nation was at war and the issue was dropped.

The opposition to deposit insurance in 1933 was understandable. Between 1908 and 1930, eight states — North Dakota, South Dakota, Nebraska, Kansas, Oklahoma, Texas, Washington and Mississippi — tried a system of deposit insurance. All went bankrupt, leaving many depositors with losses. These plans only included state-chartered banks, so they usually did not include the largest, nationally chartered banks in that state. The Secretary of the Treasury stated that it was illegal for national banks to join, because joining would be a contract to guarantee the obligations of a third party. Because most of these states were in the farm belt, the agricultural depression of the 1920s made it difficult for small banks to avoid losses.

The first plan to go bankrupt was the last one to adopt the deposit guarantee plan. Washington started the plan in 1917, and the failure of a large Seattle bank in 1921 wiped out all of the fund. In other states, such as Oklahoma and Nebraska, the depositors of the first banks to fail were reimbursed in full because the fund was able to handle that amount. It was especially noteworthy that the failure of a national bank in Superior, Nebraska, resulted in very few depositors being reimbursed, while the depositors of a state bank in that same town were reimbursed in full. This led state banks to advertise that deposits in their banks were safer than those in nationally chartered banks. But as the agricultural depression worsened in the 1920s, the state deposit insurance funds could not pay out enough to take care of the large claims, and all eight state funds were bankrupt by 1930.

Before the federal government passed a deposit insurance plan, there were several questions to be answered. Should the plan be optional or compulsory for banks? Should the premium be the same for all, or based on risk? Should private companies or the federal government be the insurer? Should the premium be based on just the amount of insured deposits or on all deposits? The final decision made the plan compulsory for member banks but optional for non-member banks. It was also decided that the federal government would not be able to evaluate risk, so a fixed premium was established. There was also the belief that if the public found out that a particular bank had to pay higher premium, there would be a rush of depositors to take their funds elsewhere. Private insurance companies showed very little interest in undertaking this coverage, so it fell to the federal government. Finally, while some in Congress felt that the large banks would indeed subsidize the smaller ones by having the premium based on all deposits rather than just the covered deposits, the small banks had a lot of influence with their congressmen and were able to get the premium based on all deposits. Some observers feared that the large banks might switch to a state charter and drop out of both the Federal Reserve system and the FDIC program, but this fear proved groundless.

The temporary plan for federal deposit insurance began in January 1934 and the permanent plan started in July 1934. The permanent plan covered each account up to $5,000 per account, which was raised over the years to the current $100,000. Each bank paid a premium of $1/12$ of 1 percent of all its deposits, not just the insured deposits. Up to half of this premium could be refunded if experience was good. Changes were made in this assessment in the late 1980s.

"Deposit insurance" was a misnomer. Real insurance firms charge according to the risk, but all banks paid the same premium. Large banks clearly subsidized the small ones, because the large banks had most of the big accounts that were beyond the amount of coverage. So this plan was a guarantee by the federal government. This was clearly shown to be the case when another deposit insurance plan, the one covering savings and loan associations, went bankrupt in the 1980s and the taxpayers had to foot the bill.

But this plan did achieve its aim of preventing bank runs. The general public now was more willing to hold deposits rather than hoard currency. The money supply could still contract from Fed policy, but no longer was hoarding of currency the cause. The plan also saved the unit bank system, which some wanted and others did not. Many observers pointed out that in Canada there were no bank failures in a system where banks could branch nationwide, and thus diversify their lending geographically and industrially. As mentioned previously, Canada suffered through the Depression along with the U.S., even though Canada had no central bank nor deposit insurance at that time.

Not only were Carter Glass and FDR opposed to deposit insurance, but initially, so were Governor Black at the Federal Reserve board and Governor George Harrison at the New York Fed. Once the law was passed, Black seemed to be supportive of it. Nevertheless, it was the work of those in Congress who represented the small banks. Since the comptroller wanted to continue to examine national banks, and the Fed wanted to keep examining state member banks, the FDIC was limited to examining the non-member banks who took out this coverage.

In addition to protecting the money supply, deposit insurance was a substitute for bank capital. A bank's capital represents the owners' equity in the bank and is a measure of how far the bank's assets (loans and securities) can fall in value and still be adequate to cover the deposits. With federal deposit insurance, depositors were much less likely to run on the bank and cause a depletion of its cash assets. After the FDIC began, bank capital, including retained earnings, became a smaller percentage of a bank's source of funds. Furthermore, the Banking Act of 1933 declared that national bank stockholders no longer had to have double liability wherein they could be assessed for an amount equal to what they had invested in bank stock. This made it easier for national banks to raise capital.

Another plan to prevent the contraction of bank deposits in a fractional reserve system, never adopted, was the proposal to require banks to hold 100 percent reserves for their checkable deposits. Several well-known economists in the 1930s, such as Irving Fisher, Milton Friedman, Lloyd Mints, Henry Simons, and Laughlin Currie, advocated this plan as a way to protect the money supply while giving the public a safe deposit. Banks would have to hold vault cash and reserves at the Fed equal to their checking deposits. The banks could get loanable funds only from non-money sources such as savings and time deposits, negotiable certificates of deposit; debentures; and capital, including retained earnings. This would also allow the Fed to increase the money supply by a steady amount because the money base and the money supply would be the same. When lending, banks would merely transfer money from themselves to the borrower, and not create money as they do now with the fractional reserve system. Banks would then be on the same footing as all other lenders who must acquire money before they can lend it: when lending, they merely transfer the ownership of the existing money supply. Bankers opposed the plan because it would affect their earnings. Irving Fisher also argued that this plan would cancel most of the national debt because the Fed would have to inject new reserves into the banking system via open market purchases, while simultaneously raising reserve requirements. With the Fed owning most of the government bonds, the debt could be nullified. But the FDIC lessened the need for such a change in banking.

Another change in the early days of the Roosevelt administration was granting the Fed the power to limit bank and non-bank lending for the purchase of securities. The stock market boom of the late 1920s was considered to be financed by too many bank loans made directly, or indirectly to brokers. Governor Black supported this measure even though he said that such restrictions in the late 1920s would not have prevented the excessive speculation. These powers were made permanent with an amendment to the Federal Reserve Act in 1935.

While the gold supply was commandeered by the Treasury in 1933, the dollar fluctuated in foreign markets until January 1934 when the government officially devalued the dollar by raising the price of gold. The gold content of the dollar was changed from 23.22 grains of pure gold to 13.714 grains, a reduction of 41 percent, or to 59 percent of its former value. The Treasury, which had forced American citizens to sell their gold for $20.67 an ounce, now reevaluated gold at $35 per ounce. From this point on, it stood ready to buy all gold mined or sent here from abroad at the $35 price, but it would only sell gold to foreigners.

While Governor Black supported some of FDR's proposals, he opposed the attempt to raise prices and wages through the National Recovery Act. So in August 1934, Black resigned intending to return to the Atlanta Fed, but he became ill and died before the year's end. In November 1934, Black was replaced by Marriner Stoddard Eccles, one of the most influential leaders the Federal Reserve board was to have until the 1950s. It was under Eccles that the Federal Reserve Act was amended, mostly by his handiwork. He became the first chairman of the board when the structure was changed, remained in this position until April 1948, and then stayed on the board until July 1951.

Eccles had only a high school education, but he had made a great deal of money managing his family business interests, which included lumber, railroading, sugar processing and banking. When the Depression began, he advocated deficit spending to increase employment, so he was a supporter more of fiscal policy than of monetary policy. He also believed that income was inequitably distributed and wanted a more equal dispersal in order to increase consumption, which he felt could not keep up with production when there were so many people at a low level of income. This made him attractive to the Roosevelt administration. When offered the post of Assistant to the Secretary of the Treasury for Monetary and Credit Affairs he accepted, intending to stay in Washington for only a year and a half. But when Black resigned as governor of the Federal Reserve board, FDR appointed Eccles to replace him. Eccles accepted under the condition that FDR would support a major reform in the Fed, which became the 1935 Amendment to the Federal Reserve Act. FDR did not consult with Carter Glass about the Eccles appointment, which led to some animosity between the senator and the new leader of the Fed. Roosevelt gave Eccles a recess appointment in November 1934 but it took until April 1935 for the Senate to approve him, with Carter Glass opposed.

The 1935 Amendment to the Federal Reserve Act placed the power in the board's hands and reduced the independence of the district banks. The Federal Open Market Committee (FOMC) had replaced the Open Market Policy Conference in 1933, but it still contained the governors of the twelve district banks on it. The 1935 Act reduced the FOMC to the seven members of the board, which was now called the Board of Governors of the Federal Reserve System, plus five others. Eccles was instrumental in removing the Secretary of the Treasury from the board; Secretary Morganthau decided that if he was going to be out, then the Comptroller of the Currency, who was under him, should leave also. Each person on the Board was a governor, so the leader was now the chairman. In addition, the FOMC consisted of the head of the New York or Boston Fed and four of the eleven heads of the other district banks. In 1942, the New York Fed became a permanent member of the FOMC, indicating its prominence. These leaders of the district banks were no longer called governors but presidents. (So the Fed is the one place where governor is higher than president.) The New York Fed was still "more equal" than the other eleven district banks because it was the only one whose president was a permanent member of the FOMC. In addition, the salary of the president of the New York Fed was higher than that of the chairman of the Board of Governors. Now all open market operations were directed by this committee, and no district bank could buy or sell for its own account. Each district bank was assigned a certain amount of securities to trade so that the system would act as a unit.

Carter Glass and Marriner S. Eccles battled over the Banking Act of 1935, with Eccles winning most of the battles. Glass wanted a decentralized Fed, not one dominated by the board. Eccles told FDR he would only take the Fed chairmanship if the act was amended to place more power in the board and less in the district banks. The only compromise to Glass was keeping some of the Reserve Bank presidents on the FOMC but the Board of Governors with seven members had the majority. Glass also lost out on the attempt to permit the Reserve Banks to opt out of any open market operations. Eccles convinced Congress that monetary policy was a national, not a regional, tool.

The amendment also gave the Board of Governors the power to raise reserve requirements to double what they had been for each class of bank: country, reserve city, and central reserve city. This power rested solely with the board and did not require approval of Congress, the President of the United States, or the district banks.

It was exercised in 1936 and 1937 with disastrous results, as will be shown.

The amendment also made permanent the power of the board to set maximum interest rates that banks could pay on time and savings accounts, called Regulation Q. The Fed had authority over all member banks, and the FDIC over state banks that took out deposit insurance. Another control exercised solely by the board, and not by the district banks, was the margin requirements on stock purchases. These two regulations, U and T, covered loans by banks for stock purchases and also loans by non-bank lenders for that purpose.

Even after pushing this bill through Congress, Eccles still had to go through senate confirmation as the chairman of the new Board of Governors. Senator Carter Glass delayed the appointment because he resented any changes from the original Federal Reserve bill, which he had largely written, that originally called for decentralized authority. Eccles was confirmed even with Glass's opposition. Now after the 1935 Act was passed, authority was clearly centered in Washington, D.C. The seven governors were given fourteen year terms that were staggered, so that an opening would occur in January of an even-numbered year. This was to prevent any president from dominating the board with his appointees. Even if an appointed governor voted in a way that the president disapproved, the governor could not be removed until the end of his term.

Another major change during the Roosevelt administration was the large inflow of gold from abroad. When the U.S. devalued the dollar by raising the price of gold to $35 an ounce, this encouraged foreign holders of gold to sell it to the U.S. Treasury. It also encouraged gold mining, and this too had to be sold to the Treasury. When the Treasury bought the gold, its check, written on its account at the Federal Reserve, was deposited into the banking system, which caused an equal increase in reserves and deposits. When the Treasury wanted this gold purchase to add to the money base and the money supply, it replenished its account at the Fed by issuing gold certificates, which the Fed held as a reserve for its reserve deposits and federal reserve notes.

The process of monetizing gold purchases by the Treasury can be seen in the following illustration:

Treasury		Federal Reserve		Banking System	
Assets	*Liabilities*	*Assets*	*Liabilities*	*Assets*	*Liabilities*
+Gold			-Treas Acct	+Res	+Deposit
-Acct at			+ Reserves		
Fed					

After the gold purchase, the Treasury replenishes its account at the Fed by issuing gold certificates, which the Fed holds as a reserve asset for the bank reserve accounts and the federal reserve notes

Treasury		Federal Reserve		Banking System	
Assets	*Liabilities*	*Assets*	*Liabilities*	*Assets*	*Liabilities*
+Acct	+Gold	+Gold	+Treas.	No change	
at Fed.	Certificates	Certificates	Dep.		

This is what mainly happened from 1934 to the end of 1936. The money base rose 60 percent in this period, and the money supply rose just 51 percent. It was the Treasury's purchase of gold that caused the large increase in the money base, not the Federal Reserve purchasing securities in the open market. Then for the first nine months of 1937 the Treasury sterilized the gold purchases. This was done by the Treasury not issuing gold certificates to replenish its account at the Fed, but instead pulling funds from its tax and loan accounts in the banking system. This caused an increase in Treasury cash, which represents the difference between the gold stock and the outstanding gold certificates. This inactive gold then does not add to the money base, as is shown below:

Treasury		Federal Reserve		Banking System	
Assets	*Liabilities*	*Assets*	*Liabilities*	*Assets*	*Liabilities*
-Tax &			- Reserves	-Res.	– Tax &.
Loan Acct			+Treasury acct		Loan Acct
+Acct at					
Fed					

During the 1934–1937 period, the economy experienced an expansion in output and prices, but unemployment still remained very high. The unemployment rate was about 11 percent in 1937, which was an improvement over 25 percent in 1933, but a long way from full employment. Critics of the Roosevelt administration blamed the high unemployment on low business investment, which they felt was discouraged by some of the anti-business measures of the New Deal. But this anemic recovery was about to be abruptly stopped.

With the money base rising 60 percent, it was unusual for the money stock to rise by only 51 percent. In the early 1930s, the public's demand for currency caused the money stock to decline. But in the period after deposit insurance started, the deposit/currency ratio remained fairly steady. The factor that caused a much smaller rise in the money stock was commercial banks' greater demand for excess reserves. The deposit/reserve ratio fell steadily from 1933 to about 1940, which meant that banks were holding very large amounts of excess reserves at the Fed. Since no interest is paid on these reserves by the Fed to the banks, it surprised Fed officials. These increased reserves resulted not from any expansionary policy by the Fed, but solely from the Treasury's gold purchases. But Eccles and other Board members believed that monetary policy had been very easy, and that these excess reserves could cause an inflationary rise in spending if banks increased their lending to the maximum.

In reality, monetary policy had *not* been easy. Open market purchases were made only to adjust the maturities of the bonds in the Fed's portfolio. There was no net increase in the amount held. The discount rate was 1.5 percent and later lowered to 1 percent, which was low compared to what it had been in the 1920s but high compared to short-term market rates on Treasury bills and commercial paper. Bank borrowing at the Fed was negligible because of the large amount of excess reserves and also because the rates on Treasury bills were a fraction of 1 percent, making it cheaper for a bank to sell them in the open market than to borrow from the Fed.

The Fed did not want to decrease bank reserves by open market sales of securities because they felt they needed the income from these bonds to pay expenses and dividends on the stock held by member banks. The Fed was still thinking of its own financial position rather than the well-being and performance of the economy. So they decided to use their newly acquired tool, changing reserve requirements. This tool, unlike discounting and open-market operations, does not change the money base; it changes the money multiplier. The money base consists of all currency and coin outside the Fed and the Treasury plus the member bank reserve deposits at the Fed. Open market purchases of securities or lending via the discount mechanism injects new reserves, hence money base, into the banking system. On the other hand, changing reserve requirements is a very blunt and powerful tool because it changes both the numerator and denominator of the deposit multiplier. Since banks can expand lending and deposits by the amount of their excess reserves divided by the reserve requirement (ER/res. req.), an increase in reserve requirements lowers the amount of excess reserves while simultaneously making them less expansionary. This tool also discriminated against member banks in the 1930s because the Fed could not change non-member bank reserve requirements until after 1980. Nevertheless, the Fed went ahead with this new tool and doubled reserve requirements in three steps: August 1936; March 1937; and May 1937. What the Fed overlooked was that banks wanted those excess reserves. They were legally excess but not economically excess.

The increases in reserve requirements on the three classes of banks, plus their time deposits, is shown in the following table:

	Central Reserve City Banks	Reserve City Banks	Country Banks	Time Deposits
To 8/15/36	13.00%	10.00%	7.00%	4.00%
8/15/36–3/1/37	19.50%	15.00%	10.50%	4.5%
3/1–5/1/37	22.75%	17.50%	12.25%	5.25%
after 5/1/37	26.00%	20.00%	14.00%	6.00%

Why would commercial banks want to hold excess reserves? In normal times, they do not, but the 1930s were not normal. The Fed was not providing for seasonal needs for currency as in the past, so banks felt they had to watch out for themselves. In addition, the bank runs of the early 1930s were a vivid memory. It is true that the FDIC worked to stop bank runs, but the banks did not know it would work as well as it did. After all, they remembered the eight state deposit insurance plans that failed in the 1920s. So banks reacted to the loss of their excess reserves by trying to reestablish them either by dumping securities on the market or by calling in loans. After the first increase in reserves in August 1936, the deposit reserve ratio dropped sharply, clearly showing the banks' reaction to that increase. But the Fed went right ahead with the next two increases. Chairman Eccles was opposed to the last increase but was outvoted.

The large banks in New York felt the impact of the increase in reserve requirements more keenly than banks in other cities because so many correspondent banks pulled their accounts out of New York. This deflationary effect was intensified when the Treasury sterilized its gold purchases. Surprisingly, George Harrison, president of the New York Fed, was for the increase in reserve requirements because once they were at the maximum, he felt the board could no longer use this tool and would have to revert to open market operations in which the district banks have a voice. But the impact on the economy was severe. The money supply had been growing at a rate of 4.2 percent per year from 1933 to June 1937, but then it dropped sharply until May 1938. The amount of money was $31.1 billion in March 1937 and only $29.1 billion in May 1938. This was accompanied by an increase in unemployment from 11 percent to 19 percent, as real income dropped 5 percent between 1937 and 1938.

In September 1937, as the recession was causing unemployment to rise, Chairman Eccles asked the Treasury to release $300 million in inactive gold. This was surprising since the Fed could have purchased that amount of bonds in the market, which would have had the same effect. Even though the Treasury did issue $300 of gold certificates, which monetized that much gold, it continued to sterilize new gold purchases until February 1939. Eccles also wanted the Fed to purchase more bonds in the open market. The Fed bought $38 million in November 1938, but no more until the middle of 1939.

Federal Reserve officials have always shifted the blame for what goes wrong in the economy to something besides their monetary actions. Eccles believed in the effectiveness of fiscal policy rather than monetary policy. He advocated large federal deficits and increased public works to reduce unemployment. He believed that monetary policy is weak when it comes to getting a country out of a depression, because the new reserves injected into the banking system may be hoarded. He used the analogy that monetary policy is like a string: you can pull on it but you cannot push on it. The large amount of excess reserves at that time only reinforced his view on this. He blamed the recession on the attempt of the Roosevelt administration to balance the budget by increasing taxes and decreasing spending. In addition, the social security tax was a regressive tax which siphoned money from even low-wage workers, but it did not inject any spending into the economy until benefits began in 1939.

Conversely, Henry Morganthau at the Treasury put the blame squarely on the Federal Reserve for doubling the reserve requirements. This clearly was a contractionary move that caused banks to try to restore these excess reserves, which were not very costly to the bank since short-term rates on securities were extremely low. As mentioned before, this tool discriminated against member banks because the Fed could not set the reserve requirements for non-member banks. The latter, however, were still adversely affected by the dumping of securities, which lowered the prices of the bonds non-member banks were holding. In addition, these non-member banks held correspondent balances in member banks, so the money-center bank could have asked for higher balances from these non-member banks, balances that were non-interest-bearing. The Fed did reduce these reserve requirements in April 1938, but this undid only about a fourth of the increases.

The bottom of the 1937–1938 recession came in mid–1938 as the economy began to recover. The impetus was not the Fed increasing the money supply by open market purchases, but the Treasury buying more gold as war clouds in Europe caused the shipment of gold to the U.S. The Treasury issued gold certificates to monetize this new gold, while the Fed engaged in open market operations only to maintain "orderly" conditions in the government bond market. The Fed wanted to prevent sharp decreases in the bonds in banks' portfolios, but usually reversed these purchases later. From 1937 to 1940, banks continued to add to their excess reserves, causing the deposit-to-reserve ratio to fall.

Banks wanted to be more liquid, and held not only more cash assets but also more securities than loans. As shown below, the percentage of assets bank held in loans fell, while the percentages held in securities and cash assets rose throughout the 1930s:

Percentage of Bank Assets

	In Loans	*In Securities*	*In Cash Assets*
1929	57.9	22	14.4
1933	40.7	34.8	18.3
1937	30.8	38.8	26.4
1939	26.7	37.5	32.4
1941	26.9	36.2	34.2

This represents a shift in bank demand for more liquidity and more safety. It could also reflect a decrease in business loan demand because of depressed conditions. But one category within securities needs explaining. In 1936, banks held more short-term Treasury bills than long-term government bonds; bonds were only 45 percent of the holdings of federal securities. When reserve requirements were doubled in 1936 and 1937, banks dumped Treasury bills on the market, causing their prices to fall. But within a short time their prices rose, and thus their yields fell to less than a tenth of 1 percent, making it too expensive for banks to re-acquire them. So by 1941, long-term government bonds were 74 percent of banks' holdings of federal securities.

The deposit-to-reserve ratio fell to its lowest in 1940, and then began to rise as banks probably did not fear bank runs as much as they had earlier. When the war started and the Fed pegged the price of government securities, it was perfectly safe for banks to hold these bonds, because they were almost like interest-bearing cash. This happened in 1942, and will be discussed in the next section.

What is somewhat paradoxical in the period since 1935 is the fact that the structure of the Federal Reserve changed with the view to make it more independent, and to place more power in the board in Washington, away from the New York money center. The latter was achieved with the board forming a majority on the FOMC and having the power to change reserve requirements and restrict lending on stocks. But the Fed did not become independent of the Treasury, even though the Secretary of the Treasury and the Comptroller of the Currency were removed from the board. It was the Treasury and not the Fed that was responsible for the increases in the money supply resulting from gold purchases. It was the Treasury, through its sterilization of gold, that reduced the impact of these purchases on bank reserves and the money supply.

The Fed could have accomplished this through open market sales, but did not want to lose the interest income. That led to the increase in reserve requirements that was the main Fed impact on the economy in the 1930s, albeit a depressing one. Then instead of buying securities in 1938 to offset the deflationary impact of the gold sterilization, the Fed asked the Treasury to issue gold certificates for some of the inactive gold it was holding. This dominance of the Treasury was to become complete during World War II and even in the years following the war. As we will see, the Fed struggled to free itself from pegging the prices of government securities for several years before finally getting its way in early 1951. So independent monetary policy could not be exercised by the Fed until the 1950s.

9

The Fed's Role in World War II

Neither the Federal Reserve nor the Treasury conducted a type of monetary policy that would be designed to change the income level or the price level during the war. Instead, the aim of both agencies was to finance the war in a manner that they thought would be least disruptive to the economy. The Treasury was buying gold and issuing gold certificates up until mid–1941, when the inflow stopped. The gold stock rose from $16.6 billion in September 1939 when the war started in Europe, to $22.7 billion in late 1941 when the U.S. entered the war. This added to banks' excess reserves, which reached about $7 billion at the end of 1940, but were lowered to about $3 billion in November 1941, when the Fed raised the reserve requirements back up to the maximum allowed (undoing the decrease of April 1938). Even if the Fed had sold off its entire portfolio of government bonds in the open market, they could not have offset even half of the excess reserves caused by the gold inflow. Only the Treasury could have counteracted this increase, by not issuing gold certificates.

When the war started in Europe in September 1939, the Fed did buy about $400 million of government bonds, but only to prevent their prices from falling. This move was reversed before the year's end. But the money supply rose by 29 percent, from September 1939 to November 1941 entirely because of the gold purchases, not because of any policy by the Fed. The wholesale price level was 23 percent higher in late

1941 than in September 1939. This may have been why the Fed raised the reserve requirements for banks, but it had little impact (unlike its deflationary effect in 1937). The Board of Governors also invoked another power Congress had given it, Regulation W, in September 1941 which allowed the imposition of consumer credit controls. The controls work by imposing a minimum down payment and setting a maximum number of monthly payments for durable goods. Such a restriction is hard to enforce with so many sellers of merchandise, and it is easy to evade. But when the U.S. entered the war at the end of 1941, few consumer durable goods were available, lessening the importance of this type of control.

In early 1942, Congress imposed price and wage controls throughout the economy as a means of combating inflation. It was obvious that shortages were going to occur, so these controls had to be accompanied by widespread rationing. This meant that shoppers had to carry ration books as well as money with them to stores. These controls held the official consumer price index to an average 4 percent increase per year until they were removed in 1946, but inflation can manifest itself in other ways. Quality can decrease, inferior materials can be substituted, or poorer services offered for the same price. Where shortages did exist, rationing sometimes led to illegal dealings in black markets.

The Federal Reserve announced in April 1942 that it would cooperate with the Treasury to keep its cost of borrowing low. To accomplish this, the Fed stated it would step in and buy Treasury securities to prevent their prices from falling. If the market prices of older bonds were allowed to fall, the Treasury could not sell new ones without paying a higher interest rate. The rates on these securities varied according to maturity. Ninety-day bills were pegged at ⅜ of 1 percent while long term bonds were pegged at 2½ percent. Other rates were established for maturities in between those extremes. The problem with this arrangement was that with the Fed standing ready to buy at par any securities that the public did not want to hold, long-term bonds were as liquid as 90 day Treasury bills. In fact, these bonds were like interest bearing cash. Banks could hold long term bonds as secondary reserves, and no longer needed excess reserves at the Fed. The Fed ended up with most of the short-term issues while banks and other financial institutions, such as insurance companies, held the long-term bonds. The Fed, however, had no obligation to step in and sell bonds to keep their prices from rising (yields falling), as happened in 1944, when the long term rate dropped below 2½ percent for a time.

The above bonds were in $1000 minimums so were not targeted for consumers. To encourage the average person to help finance the war effort, Series E bonds were sold to the general public. These bonds were in denominations as low as $25; they were sold at 75 percent of face value and rose gradually to face value over ten years. The yield was only about 2.9 percent per year, but these bonds could be cashed in any time after six months at a determined price, so there was no market risk to the general public for holding these bonds. In future years when interest rates became higher, the Treasury adjusted the yield on these savings bonds by shortening the time to maturity, but kept the same purchase price at 75 percent of face value.

The increase in government spending during the war had to be financed by increases in taxes, by borrowing, or by increases in the public's willingness to hold money. Therefore, the increase in the money supply had to equal the increase in government spending minus increases in taxes and increases in borrowing by bond sales. But since an increase in the money supply is equal to increases in demand deposits plus the increase in currency holdings, the Fed had to take into consideration the deposit-to-reserve ratios and the deposits-to-currency ratios the banks and the public desired. If the public wanted more currency, more base money would have to be created. As it turned out, the increase in the government's wartime spending was financed 48 percent by taxes, 31 percent by interest-bearing government bonds, 14 percent by banks' money creation via bond buying, and 7 percent by pure Fed money creation.

When the Fed agreed to pegging the prices of government securities, it lost all control over the supply of money. It was under an obligation to create the amount of base money (currency and reserve deposits) needed to keep the prices of the bonds fixed. The Fed itself bought some issues directly from the Treasury, which it cannot do now; permission was given by Congress because of the emergency. This is a pure printing of money, because the Fed takes the bonds as an asset and credits the Treasury's account at the Fed. When the Treasury spends the new funds, they come into the banking system as newly created deposits and reserves. Since banks need to hold only a fraction of these reserves for the new deposits, most of the reserves are excess that can be used for further lending and money creation. This situation is illustrated below:

Treasury		Federal Reserve		Banking System	
Assets	*Liabilities*	*Assets*	*Liabilities*	*Assets*	*Liabilities*
+Acct	+Bonds	+Bonds	+Treas	no change yet	
at Fed			Acct		

Then the Treasury spends the newly created money:

Treasury		Federal Reserve		Banking System	
Assets	*Liabilities*	*Assets*	*Liabilities*	*Assets*	*Liabilities*
-Acct			-Treas	+Res.	+Deposits
At Fed			Acct		
+Goods			+Reserves		

Conversely, when the Treasury taxes the public to finance its spending, no money is created and the public loses the purchasing power the government gains. If the Treasury sells bonds to the public, no money is created in this case either. Spending power is transferred as with taxes, but the public gets an interest-earning asset instead of a tax receipt. If bonds are sold to commercial banks, new money is created in the same manner as if the bank bought a private bond or made a loan to a company, but with a limited amount of reserves the Treasury is using funds that might have been lent to firms.

When members of the non-bank public buy bonds, funds are transferred from checking accounts to the Treasury's Tax & Loan and thus are kept in the banking system. When the Treasury decides to spend these funds, it moves them up to its account at the Federal Reserve. After the checks are written, they return to the banking system, leaving it with the same amount of reserves and deposits as before the borrowing. This is shown below:

Federal Reserve		Banking System	
Assets	*Liabilities*	*Assets*	*Liabilities*
			- Deposits
			+ Tax & Loan

The Treasury then moves the funds to its account at the Fed:

Federal Reserve		Banking System	
Assets	*Liabilities*	*Assets*	*Liabilities*
	+Treas Acct	-Reserves	-Tax & Loan
	-Reserves		

After the Treasury spends these funds, the money remains the same because the Treasury spent the money the public was holding.

Federal Reserve		Banking System	
Assets	*Liabilities*	*Assets*	*Liabilities*
	-Treas Acct	+Res.	+Deposits
	+Reserves		

Because of the importance of World War II, the Federal Reserve was mainly concerned with helping the Treasury finance the war. As the Treasury's fiscal agent, the Fed believed this was more important than preventing inflation. Board of Governors Chairman Marriner Eccles, along with governors John McKee and Ernest Draper, formed the War Loans Committee, which was designed to supervise the activities of the Fed with regard to financing the war, and to gather information regarding potential postwar problems. There was a fear that the low interest rates that helped finance the war could lead to postwar inflation, or if bond rates were allowed to rise, this would create capital losses for banks and firms holding government bonds. The Board of Governors wanted Congress to impose special scurity reserve requirements on commercial banks against their demand deposits. The Fed thought that this requirement would create a better market for government bonds after the war and allow the Fed to maintain lower interest rates, which would avoid capital losses for bond holders. However, Congress refused to implement the Fed's request because many commercial banks opposed being forced to hold government securities once the war was over.

World War II was such a large undertaking that government deficits reached levels that had never been seen up until that time. The tax receipts and expenditures by the federal government and the resulting deficits are shown below:

Year	Receipts	Expenditures	Deficits
1942	14,634	35,137	20,503
1943	24,001	78,555	54,554
1944	43,747	91,304	47,557
1945	45,159	92,712	47,553

The figures are in millions of dollars, so the total deficits in those four war years came to $170,167,000,000. In other words, in 1945 the government spent $92.7 billion but took in only $45.1 billion in taxes, adding $47.5 billion to the national debt. About 48 percent of the war was paid for in taxes, leaving the rest to be financed by borrowing and money creation, as mentioned above.

The money supply rose from about $29 billion in late 1941 to $102 billion by the war's end in September 1945. One factor besides price controls that held down inflation was the public's increased holding of currency, which amounted to about $17 billion. This factor prevents the supply of money from rising because currency uses reserves dollar for dollar, whereas bank deposits are fractionally backed. The deposit/currency ratio fell from 6:1 to 4:1 from November 1941 to January 1946. However, one factor working to increase the money supply was the rise in the deposit/reserve ratio by banks, which increased from 4:1 in November 1941 to 6:1 in January 1946. The wholesale price level rose only 14 percent during the war period, or about 4 percent per year. Without price controls, such a large increase in the money supply would have seen a much larger change in the price index.

The public held more money during the war, and money could be either currency or deposits in banks. In 1945, money balances were 69 percent of national income, which meant that velocity, (the number of times a given money supply is spent in a year), was less than 2. From 1942 to 1946, velocity declined by one-third. There is no apparent reason for this because other safe assets, such as Series E bonds, FDIC-insured savings deposits, and postal savings were available to the general public. The public may have held the extra money to engage in the black market, to avoid high taxes, or because they expected the postwar period to be one of depression and deflation, as in the 1930s. But the decline in velocity (which was an increase in the demand to hold money) was another factor in keeping prices as low as they were during the war.

With the large increase in deposits and currency, the Fed was again running short of gold certificates to hold as a reserve for federal reserve notes and member bank reserve deposits. In May 1944, the FOMC voted to reallocate gold certificates among the twelve Federal Reserve Banks so that each would have enough to meet the 40 percent requirements for federal reserve notes and the 35 percent requirement for member bank reserve deposits. The banks with low gold reserves sold Treasury bills to those with adequate reserves for more gold certificates. But with the money supply continuing to grow, gold reserves were becoming low. Therefore, the Fed asked Congress to lower the reserve requirement to 25 percent for both liabilities. Marriner Eccles wanted to drop the gold requirement altogether, but others at the Fed felt the public would not accept that because they wanted some tie to gold. Legislation was introduced to lower these gold reserve requirements in January 1945; the bill was passed and signed by President Truman in June. That same law also extended the provision of the 1932 Glass Steagall Act to permit the use of Treasury securities to serve as collateral for federal reserve notes. Since government obligations could now back regular federal reserve notes instead of commercial paper as the 1913 Act had required, use of the emergency currency (the Federal Reserve Bank Note) became unnecessary. So those that remained in circulation were retired, with the Treasury assuming obligation for them.

One other role the Fed played during World War II was to try to get agreements among other nations about the type of international financial system the world was going to adopt after the war. The governor on the board with the most expertise in international economic affairs was Menc Stephen Szymczak, who had been appointed to the old Federal

Reserve board in June 1933. When the new board of Governors was created by the Banking Act of 1935, only he and Marriner Stoddard Eccles were reappointed to the new Board. In 1944, Szymczak served as chairman of the U.S. Mission to London for Foreign Economic Administration for the Reconstruction of Postwar Belgium. He also was the Fed's advisor to the International Monetary and Financial Conference that was held at Bretton Woods, New Hampshire, that same year. This was the conference that set up the International Monetary Fund (IMF), which established fixed exchange rates based on gold, or on the U.S. dollar as a reserve currency. However, neither the Fed nor the Bank of England were the main architects of this scheme. Rather, the conference was run by U.S. Treasury and British Treasury officials. The British wanted to avoid their interwar problems of returning to the pre–1914 gold standard by having to deflate domestically to adopt their price level to the fixed exchange rate for balance of payments equilibrium.

The IMF was designed to allow a nation's international policy to adjust to its domestic price level, either by borrowing from surplus nations to meet a temporary imbalance, or by devaluing its currency if there was a fundamental problem. With the United States defining its dollar as equal to $35 an ounce of gold, many nations used American dollars to settle international balance of payments. But as U.S. deficits became larger in the 1960s, the supply of dollars on the world market exceeded the amount of gold valued at that price. This system was flawed because it allowed a nation to follow its own expansionary domestic policy and then devalue its currency, putting the cost of adjustment on others. With exchange rates supposedly fixed, it led to destabilizing speculation in the foreign exchange market. If a particular currency was under pressure and seemed to be facing devaluation, speculators had everything to gain and nothing to lose. They could dump the weak currency and buy a stronger one, and would lose nothing if the weak currency somehow avoided devaluation. But they stood to make a big profit if their guess was right. Under today's rules of floating rates, speculation tends to be more stabilizing. During the height of World War II in 1944, this system was probably the best that could be agreed upon, but it caused a drain on the U.S. gold supply and finally ended in 1971.

10

The Fed Between World War II and the Korean War

Many well-known economists who were influenced by the Depression-era writings of John Maynard Keynes predicted that the U.S. would have great difficulty in maintaining full employment after the war. Some of Keynes' followers, such as Professor Alvin Hansen, Abba Lerner, and Paul Samuelson, were worried about the public saving too much, making it difficult to find investment outlets for this saving. There was also a fear of converting from a wartime economy to a peace-time economy, and a belief that discharged servicemen would have trouble finding employment. Keynes, a British economist, seemed to favor the use of fiscal policy rather than monetary policy, as the main instrument to influence the level of national income. Fiscal policy is the use of government spending and taxing to exert a direct impact on total spending. The Keynesian school of thought relegated monetary policy to the role of making the supply of money available for borrowing for investment by keeping interest rates low. This school of thought considered the impact of money to be on interest rates, rather than on spending directly.

As a consequence of the prolonged depression of the 1930s, Congress passed the Employment Act of 1946 which specifically made it federal government policy to use its resources to assure that there would be "...maximum employment, production and purchasing power..." to prevent a repeat of the 1930s. Most congressmen probably were

85

thinking that fiscal measures of government spending would have to be increased if private spending were insufficient to provide full employment. But in the postwar period, private spending did prove to be adequate while the federal government ran surpluses, thus retiring some of its debt.

Because of this law, Congress set up a Joint Economic Committee and established for the President a Council of Economic Advisors. The assumption was that these new committees would be needed to deal with the complex issues that would arise when the economy was not performing well. President Truman, therefore, was the first president to have a Council of Economic Advisors, but he did not consult his economists very often.

The price controls imposed during the war suppressed inflation. When they were removed in June 1946, inflation increased but not as much as economists expected. Gold flowed into the country after the war, but this addition to the money base was offset largely by reductions in fiat money the Treasury had issued during the war. This fiat money, primarily consisted of Federal Reserve Bank Notes, the same special currency that had been issued during the First World War and again in 1933 (because it did not require the 40 percent backing in gold that the federal reserve notes did). As mentioned in the previous chapter, Congress reduced the gold reserve requirements both for federal reserve notes and for member bank reserve deposits at the Fed to 25 percent in 1945.

In addition to the inflow of gold, the Federal Reserve was still obligated to peg the prices of Treasury securities. This meant that if banks, insurance companies, and other firms wanted to sell them, which is what happened, then the Fed had to step in and buy as many as it took to prevent their prices from falling, i.e., their yields from rising. These involuntary open market purchases added about $11 billion to the money base between the end of the war and July 1946. After that month, these bond purchases slowed somewhat, adding only $5.3 billion to the base from July 1946 to May 1947. Nevertheless, the wholesale price index rose by 16.4 percent from January 1946 to August 1948. Part of that increase can be accounted for by the removal of price controls in June 1946. The money supply, defined as currency held by the public and both checking and savings accounts at commercial banks, rose from $132.5 billion to $147.1 billion between those same two months (an increase of 11 percent). But the increase in the money supply was not smooth: it increased by 8.6 percent from August 1945 to July 1946; by 3.8 percent from that point until May 1947; and then by only 1.8 percent from then until January 1948, the highest point until May 1950.

The increase in the price level, along with pressure by the Treasury to continue to support the prices of its securities, caused a great deal of concern among the Board of Governors of the Federal Reserve System. Marriner Eccles was still the chairman until February 1948, but his strong statements that the Fed should not continue to peg the prices of Treasury securities did not endear him to President Truman. Truman was a populist who believed interest rates should be kept low to make it easier for people to borrow. Truman remembered his experience in World War I when he bought some Liberty bonds in the first bond drive, but suffered a capital loss when he sold them after the war. The reason was that the Liberty bonds sold in the next bond drive were offered at a higher interest rate, thus causing Truman's bonds to fall in market value when he sold them before the maturity date. Truman did not want federal bond holders to experience capital losses. However, the marketable bonds sold during World War II were in denominations of $1000 or above, and not likely to be held by most families. Small savers had Series E bonds, which did thus not fluctuate in market value.

Eccles was worried much more about postwar inflation (because of the Fed pegging bond prices) than about the possibility of large-scale unemployment that concerned Keynesian economists. To counter the threatened inflation, Eccles wanted price controls to be kept along with wartime rationing, as well as curbs on consumer and stock market credit. He was also disappointed that the excess profits tax was repealed and that the War Labor Board was abolished. His reasoning was somewhat paradoxical. He recognized that price and wage controls caused lower quality goods and hoarding of labor services, but he seemed to ignore the fact that an excess profit tax can slow much needed investment. Eccles also disregarded the efficiency of the free market system in emitting accurate price signals, a process crucial to allocating resources in the most effective manner.

The price and wage controls of World War II caused employers of large companies to offer non-cash payments to get scarce employees, thus evading these controls. But we are still living today with the consequences of these controls. It became commonplace for firms to offer health and retirement benefits in lieu of pay increases benefits that now have become crucial to a worker selecting a place to work. But this discriminates against independent workers and owners of small firms. In addition, these benefits, along with more recent government impositions such as requirements to offer family leave and hire people with disabilities, have made it more expensive for firms to hire workers. They often find it less expensive to pay overtime to existing employees than to hire new ones.

Because of the disagreement between Truman and Eccles, the president appointed Thomas McCabe to the Board of Governors when a vacancy occurred in January 1948. McCabe had been president of Scott Paper Company and chairman of the board of directors of the Federal Reserve Bank of Philadelphia. Truman made it clear he was going to make McCabe the chairman as soon as the Senate approved his appointment, which took over two months. But Eccles' term as a governor on the board did not expire until 1951, so he chose to remain on the Board where he continued to speak out against pegging bond prices and an easy money policy. Eccles was the last chairman of the Board of Governors to remain on the board after he was removed from the chairmanship.

Both Eccles and McCabe were concerned with fighting inflation. Since the Fed could not engage in open market sales while pegging government bond prices, Congress gave the Fed special permission to raise reserve requirements temporarily in 1948. The reserve requirement for demand deposits went to 30 percent, in central reserve cities to 24 percent in reserve city banks, and to 18 percent in country banks. Time deposits at all banks were increased to 7½ percent. This special permission for these high reserve requirements expired in June 1949, and Congress did not renew it even though Chairman McCabe asked for it to continue. Congress was sensitive to commercial bank objections to tying up such a large percentage of their assets in non-earning form. McCabe also wanted the Fed to have control over reserve requirements for all banks not just member banks, but that was also denied to him. That power would not be given the Fed until after a major change in 1980.

The Federal Reserve did not compile money supply statistics until much later. Therefore, it was unaware that the money supply peaked in January 1948 and from there declined until November 1949. This decline was not as sharp as the sharp drop in the 1929–1933 period or the 1937–1938 decline, but a mild recession followed. The Fed was still fighting inflation, not only with the increased reserve requirements but also with an increase in the discount rate. The latter, however, was mainly symbolic. Banks had not been borrowing from the Fed at the discount window since the early 1930s, because they had a lot of excess reserves and could sell bonds that were pegged in price by the Fed to get needed reserves. In addition, short term rates in the market were lower than the discount rate, making it unprofitable for banks to borrow from the Fed. But a significant move by the Fed did work to slow down the expansion, and even move the economy into a slump.

From November 1947 until March 1948, the Fed bought $5 million of long-term government bonds, to keep the interest rate at 2½ percent, but simultaneously sold $6 million of short-term Treasury bills. This reduced the amount of Federal Reserve credit in the economy by a million dollars, while reserve requirements were increased. The Fed and the Treasury agreed to allow the price of ninety-day Treasury bills and one-year certificates to fall, which increased their yields to 1⅛ and 1¼ percent respectively. But the Treasury was adamant that the rate on long-term bonds remain fixed at 2½ percent. This temporary agreement between the two agencies may have been prompted by the Fed starting in April 1947 to turn over 90 percent of its earnings to the Treasury. This income was practically all from the interest on the government bonds in its portfolio. When the Fed paid the dividends on its stock to member banks, and paid its employees and other expenses, it was using only about 10 percent of its income, so this move reduced the interest cost of the federal debt.

The recession of late 1948 and early 1949 was mild and ended with an upsurge in October. One reason this recession was short and mild was that although there was a decline in the money supply of about 1½ percent, the rate at which the public spent money (velocity) dropped only slightly in 1949 before rising briskly. During the expansion of 1946 to 1948, the public's holding of money dropped from 10.3 months of national income to 9.2 months. This increased only to 9.5 months in the 1949 recession before dropping sharply to 7.9 months in 1951. What was true of money was also true of other liquid assets such as savings bonds, postal savings, and deposits in savings banks and savings and loan associations. Even though the public was gradually spending down some of its liquid assets, it was holding more than usual, perhaps because some economists had predicted a postwar depression. But after the mild 1949 recession and the outbreak of the Korean War, this expectation changed dramatically, and velocity rose sharply as the public did spend down its cash balances and other liquid assets.

The Federal Reserve was also concerned with excessive consumer spending in the postwar period. One governor, Rudolph M. Evans, was particularly outspoken on the need to control consumer credit. The Fed controlled consumer credit during the war with Regulation W, which set minimum down payments and a maximum number of months in which to pay for a consumer durable good. This control was allowed to lapse in November 1947, but Evans testified before Congress in August 1948 for its reinstatement. Evans believed that purchasing consumer durables on easy credit can get both the buyer and the seller into overextended positions. Evans rejected the idea that the government should not protect people from their own folly; he believed that regulations on credit can bring about greater economic stability, which is in keeping with the Employment Act of 1946. Some credit controls were reinstated during the Korean War, as we will see in the next chapter.

11

The Korean War and the Accord with the Treasury

Perhaps the opening round of the battle between the Fed and the Treasury was fired in June 1949 when the FOMC announced as a new policy that it would conduct open market operations with primary regard to business conditions. Chairman Thomas McCabe believed this statement was necessary to release the Fed from the straitjacket of having to peg the prices of long-term government bonds. Later that year McCabe appeared before the joint economic committee chaired by Senator Paul Douglas of Illinois, a former economics professor at the University of Chicago, and was asked if price flexibility meant both ways. In June 1949 the economy was in the mild 1949 recession, and the long term rate on government bonds actually fell below the 2½ percent pegged rate. The Treasury had no objection to a lower long-term rate, but Senator Douglas asked Chairman McCabe if the Fed would allow prices of government bonds to be flexible downward (i.e. their rates of interest to rise) if an inflationary situation should arise in the future. McCabe said yes, the prices have to be flexible in both directions, but Senator Douglas wondered if the Treasury understood this.

It emerged that the Treasury did *not* understand what McCabe meant. When the Korean War began in June 1950, inflationary pressures surged as consumers went on a buying spree for durable goods. Consumers feared that durable goods would not be available as in the case of World War II, which was vivid in the public's memory. While the Korean War was not like the total war of the early 1940s, the public did not know that at the onset. In late 1941 and early 1942 most consumers did not have the money to buy cars, refrigerators, stoves and other durable goods, but in 1950 they did. The Fed did not follow an easy money policy, but the public financed its purchases by decreasing its holdings of cash and other liquid assets. This means that velocity rose, which can cause an increase in money income for a short time. (By itself, velocity could not cause a permanent increase in spending.)

To try to combat the increase in consumer spending, the Fed reestablished consumer credit controls by setting a minimum down payment and fixing a maximum number of monthly payments for a given contract in September 1950. The Fed set new real estate credit controls in October. They also increased the margin requirements on stock purchases from 50 percent to 75 percent in January 1951. The Federal Reserve Board still had many strong advocates of specific controls that could impact various sectors of the economy. Governor Rudolph M. Evans, as mentioned before, was especially vocal in his advocacy of controlling consumer credit, particularly after the surge in buying that followed the start of the Korean War. He made speeches before the American Bankers Association in St. Louis and before the Tri-Convention in Atlantic City arguing that sellers should not compete on the basis of generous credit terms because sellers, as well as buyers, can get themselves into over-extended positions with easy credit. When the Board of Governors voted in February 1951 to exempt the down payment restriction on any credit contract of less than three months, Rudolph Evans was the only governor to vote against it.

The Treasury had to refund some of its debt in September and October 1950, and the Fed was pressured to buy what private investors did not want to hold. The Fed simultaneously sold short-term Treasury bills and certificates. Nevertheless, the Fed's holdings of government securities increased by $2.4 billion from June 1950 to the end of the year. With an increase in velocity, personal income rose 22 percent the last half of 1950, as did wholesale prices. But the Treasury had more refunding of its debt to undertake in December and in January 1951. The Treasury offered five-year notes at a 1¾ percent rate but the market rejected them, forcing the Fed to buy them.

Secretary of the Treasury John Snyder in a public speech stated that the Federal Reserve would guarantee that the yield on long-term Treasury bonds would remain fixed at 2½ percent because Chairman McCabe had agreed to this. McCabe, the entire FOMC, including former chairman Eccles, strongly disagreed with Snyder, and to show their opposition allowed the long term rate to rise to 2¾ percent in January 1951. This got the attention of President Harry Truman. In an unprecedented move, he summoned the entire FOMC to the White House hoping to convince them of the importance of keeping the prices of long-term government bonds at par. Truman stated that the Fed officials had agreed to his wishes of preventing the long-term rate from rising, but McCabe and other members of the FOMC did not agree with Truman's view. McCabe sent a letter to the president stating that continued pegging the prices of those bonds would be inflationary and could adversely affect the government's financing of the Korean War. McCabe also told Secretary Snyder that the Fed would no longer support the prices of these bonds if it conflicted with the Fed's anti-inflation policy.

President Truman then formed a committee to work out a compromise. This committee consisted of McCabe; his economic advisor, Winfield Reifler; the members of the Council of Economic Advisors and the Secretary of the Treasury. But with John Snyder in the hospital, Under Secretary of the Treasury William McChesney Martin attended in his place. Martin was soon to replace McCabe as chairman of the Board of Governors at the Fed, and become the longest-reigning chairman and most influential Fed official up until that time. To avoid outside interference and possible congressional action, the two sides worked out an accord on March 4, 1951, which stated:

> The Treasury and the Federal Reserve System have reached full accord with respect to debt management and monetary policies to be pursued in furthering their common purpose to assure the successful financing of the Government's requirements and at the same time, to minimize monetization of the public debt.

This was a clear step in the Fed's drive for full monetary independence from the Treasury, but it was not the final step. In April 1951, the Treasury exchanged a 2½ percent bond for a 2¾ percent bond and the Fed did give the Treasury some support, but at declining prices. The Korean War was still going on, so the Fed did not ignore the Treasury's needs for financing its debt.

Thomas McCabe was told by President Truman that his service was not satisfactory and he would not be reappointed to the chairmanship. McCabe resigned just as the accord was announced. He was replaced by William McChesney Martin, but Martin was not Truman's man either as he continued the tight money efforts of his predecessor. In fact, Martin, who was to serve for 19 years under five presidents, was not any president's man. It took about two years after the accord for the Fed to be completely independent. By then, the Treasury was under the Eisenhower administration. The new Secretary of the Treasury, George Humphrey, advocated unsupported markets for government bonds and said that the Treasury was willing to pay whatever was needed to sell its debt. Martin stated that full Fed independence was an evolutionary process. It was in September 1953 (after the Korean War truce) that the Fed finally felt it never again had to support the prices of government securities.

The Treasury had been the active monetary policymaker since the 1933 crisis even though the 1935 Amendment to the Federal Reserve Act gave the Board of Governors control over the district Federal Reserve Banks as to how monetary policy should be conducted. But after the accord and after the Korean War, the Federal Reserve under William McChesney Martin was now taking charge of monetary policy. Pegging was a thing of the past. Even though the Fed held $1.3 billion more federal securities in December 1952 than in March 1951, Treasury bills were now yielding 2 percent and long term bonds, 2¾ percent. The Eisenhower administration wanted sound money, and in April 1953 the Treasury offered long-term bonds at 3¼ percent. When Chairman Martin stated that the commercial banks should not rely on the Fed in the fall for an increase in their reserves, the banks dumped a large amount of government bonds and even the new 3¼ percent bond fell below par.

With pegging gone, the old original tool of the Federal Reserve came back into play. Banks began borrowing from the Fed through the discount mechanism for the first time in over 17 years. Banks could no longer dump bonds with no risk and get an equal increase in their reserve accounts. But in the 1950s this original tool, while still referred to as discounting, was actually an advance. Banks no longer brought commercial paper to their district Federal Reserve Bank for an increase in their reserve account, but instead received an increase in that account on their own note secured by government securities in their portfolio. When the Fed cut the discount rate from this point on, it was no longer a symbolic gesture but did in fact affect what member banks had to pay for funds borrowed.

Reserve requirements, which had been raised to the maximum because of pegging, were decreased in July 1953 and three times in 1954 because the economy began to slow down in late 1953 and early 1954. This was one factor in increasing the deposit/reserve ratio, while another was the change in the Federal Reserve's Regulation Q, which allowed commercial banks to pay higher interest rates on time deposits in January 1954. In addition, the discount rate was reduced three times in 1954.

As a consequence of being freed from pegging the price of Treasury bonds, the Fed took upon itself a new goal, which was to provide an adequate growth of the money stock consistent with the growth of output, without inflation. This was to be an active monetary policy without regard to the Treasury's financing needs. Chairman Martin did not specify exactly what this growth rate of money should be. He did, however, often state that the Fed should "lean against the wind," implying a counter-cyclical policy, which was controversial because of the problem of recognizing when to change policy.

12

"Bills Only" as an Act
of Independence

William McChesney Martin finished the remaining four and a half years of Thomas McCabe's term as board chairman, and then was appointed to a full fourteen-year term by President Eisenhower. His term on the board expired in 1970, but presidents Kennedy and Johnson also renewed his appointment as chairman, which came up for renewal every four years. Martin gained fame as the "Boy Wonder of Wall Street" when he became the first full-time paid president of the New York Stock Exchange in 1938 at the age of 31. After Martin served in the army in World War II, President Truman appointed him to head the Export-Import Bank. Truman later asked him to serve as Assistant Secretary of the Treasury, where as mentioned, he helped bring about the accord.

Martin was not an economist and often had to endure criticism from academic economists from both the conservative and the liberal sides during his long term. Martin remarked that he relied on economists as a drunk does a light post, for support but not for illumination. One of his first moves attracted more criticism from the liberal, Keynesian economists than from the conservative side.

This controversial move was to announce that the Fed would now conduct open market operations in Treasury bills only and not in longer-term securities. Martin's reason for this was that the purpose of open market operations was to change bank reserves and hence the potential money supply, and not to change interest rates. Reserves would change the same if the Fed bought $2 million of bills or if they bought $2 million of long term bonds. Under no circumstances did Martin want the Fed to get trapped into another bond support program, as had happened from 1942 to 1951. Martin also wanted the free market to determine the structure of interest rates. He felt that the "bills only" policy would protect government bond dealers against arbitrary actions of the Fed. In addition, sales of long-term securities might cause further expectations of changes in future interest rates During the Eisenhower administration, the Fed actually deviated from the "bills only" policy three times, (November 1955, July 1958, and November 1960), ostensibly to prevent disorderly conditions in the Treasury bond market.

The liberal school of economists in the postwar period were usually disciples of British economist John Maynard Keynes, who suggested the use of government fiscal policy to achieve full employment. Most Keynesians felt that monetary policy should be secondary to fiscal policy and that the main influence of monetary policy is its effect on interest rates, which affect private investment. Thus, if the Fed were to buy long-term bonds it would increase their price, which would lower their yield and allow competing private bonds to be sold at lower interest rates. Paul Samuelson, a noted liberal economist, questioned why the Fed should give up the freedom to influence the whole spectrum of interest rates by limiting itself to "bills only." He also questioned whether changes in short-term interest rates would influence changes in long-term rates and hence in investment. He pointed out that in the 1930s short-term rates were almost zero, but long-term rates came down very slowly.

Conversely, the conservative economists generally followed the older quantity theory, which states that changes in the money supply affect spending directly, rather than having to first affect interest rates. So the Keynesian economists were concerned mainly with credit conditions, while the quantity theorists were concerned with the money supply and its impact on spending. Therefore, the quantity theorists would generally support bills only because they would be less concerned about changes in the interest rate and would look at how open market operations affect the money supply.

Another important person who objected to the bills only policy because he believed that the Fed was abdicating its power to affect the whole spectrum of interest rates was Allan Sproul, President of the New York Federal Reserve Bank. Sproul may have resented the power shift to the Board of Governors and away from the New York Fed where open market operations are conducted. In any case, he agreed with Paul Samuelson that the influences from the short-term securities market may not always connect to the long-term market. But Martin won his case and Sproul left the New York Fed in 1956.

Martin's style was opposite to that of Marriner S. Eccles, the Fed's leader from 1935 to 1948. Eccles spoke first in FOMC meetings and almost dared others to disagree, whereas Martin listened to the views of the others before speaking and giving his ideas. Martin also instituted the practice of having all twelve district bank presidents attend the FOMC meetings, even though only five of the twelve present could vote.

Martin also had disagreements with modern quantity theory economists, who found fault with Martin's advocacy of the Fed "leaning against the wind." Such a policy implied that the Fed would follow an easy money policy when a recession appeared, and pursue a tight money policy when the economy overheated to the point of inflation. These economists disagreed with this policy because they felt the Fed could not recognize when the economy was slowing down or heating up until the need was too late to act. They believed that there was a lag from the time a policy was needed until it was recognized by the Fed. There was then a shorter lag between the time the Fed recognized the need and the time they took action, which would be at the next meeting of the FOMC. Finally, these quantity theorists believed that the final lag would occur between the time action was taken and the time it impacted the economy.

They showed how the Fed, in the 1950s, acted "too much, too late" during each expansion and during each contraction. The first expansionary peak occurred in July 1953, but the Fed was following a tight money policy beyond that month, causing the recession to be deeper. The trough was reached in August 1954, but by then the Fed was following an expansionary policy that continued well into the recovery.

The next inflationary peak was July 1957, but the Fed did not recognize the need for a change until three months later. When it tightened, the economy had already entered the 1957–1958 recession, the severest since World War II up until that time. The trough of that downturn occurred in April 1958. While the Fed was by then in expansionary mode, this easy money period was abruptly stopped in September 1959, which was followed by the recession of late 1960–1961. Vice President Nixon, who was running for president in the fall of 1960, called Martin and blamed him for his narrow defeat because of the recession. Four key industrial states (Minnesota, Michigan, Missouri and Illinois) were won by President Kennedy by a relatively small percentage of votes, which might have gone the other way had not the economy been in a recession. In 1970, President Nixon would not reappoint Martin as chairman of the Board of Governors.

The modern quantity theorists, soon to be called monetarists, wanted the Fed to give up counter-cyclical monetary policy, what Martin called "leaning against the wind," and rely instead on a constant-growth-of-money rule. They believed that in this manner, money would be less of a source of disturbance and would not make cycles worse. All central bankers oppose this rule because it would take away their discretion and reduce their position to a mere mechanical one akin to that of the Bureau of Engraving, which prints currency as the economy demands it but has no say in how much should be in circulation at any time.

Another problem with the government bond market appeared in the 1950s: the ceiling of 4¼ percent that was imposed on any Treasury bond over five years maturity. This restriction had been passed during World War I, and Congress was reluctant to change it. Of course, from the early 1930s until the mid–1950s this was no problem because the legal ceiling was above market rates, even when pegging stopped. But by 1958 market rates rose above this, causing the Treasury to sell shorter-term securities than they wanted. One method used was to allow the bonds to be sold at a discount from the face value, which increased the yield to the competitive rate. Another option was presented by Secretary of the Treasury Robert B. Anderson, when he devised his "magic fives." These Treasury notes were to mature in four years and eleven months, and carried a 5 percent coupon. That issue was very successful, selling out almost immediately. Some economists who opposed the "bills only" policy argued that there might have been no need to sell these 5 percent securities. For instance, if the Fed had been willing to operate in all sectors and had supported the long-term bond market with swapping operations, that would have kept the long-term rate below the 4¼ percent ceiling. It would be some years before the Treasury could legally sell long-term bonds at a higher rate than the 4¼ percent ceiling.

Another factor affecting monetary policy in the late 1950s was the outflow of gold that began in February 1958. As in the 1930s, the Fed had been willing to allow inflows of gold to occur without impacting the money supply, but it reacted very strongly to outflows. So throughout 1958, the Fed bought enough Treasury bills to offset the decrease in the money base that the gold sales would have caused. The discount rate was increased in several steps to 4 percent. This increase served also as an attempt to encourage foreign nations to keep short-term, interest-bearing deposits here, rather than convert them to gold.

During World War II, the United States took the lead in planning a postwar system of international payments that would be based on gold but would allow for some increase in the medium of exchange beyond the amount of gold stock. This system, worked out at Bretton Woods, New Hampshire, set up the International Monetary Fund that would allow deficit nations to borrow from surplus countries. As mentioned earlier, the Fed's main representative at this conference was Governor Menc Stephen Szymczak, the Fed's expert on international affairs. A chief feature of the postwar international payments system was to use the American dollar, which was convertible into gold at $35 per ounce by non–Americans, as a reserve currency. That meant that the U.S. had to run a deficit in its balance of payments to provide a supply of dollars on the international exchange for the other nations to use. The U.S. had a very large amount of gold when the war ended, so the foreign traders were confident that they could exchange these dollars for gold whenever they wished. But after 1958 and continuing all through the 1960s, the supply of American dollars on the world market kept increasing until there were far more dollars in the hands of foreigners than the supply of U.S. gold valued at $35 per ounce. This threatened the system of fixed exchange rates. Some American economists advocated letting the dollar fluctuate freely in international markets. The government rejected this idea, either because it believed the world had become accustomed to fixed exchange rates, or because it believed who those nations that held the dollars without demanding gold would be adversely affected if the dollar fell in relation to other currencies. So the gold outflow was to be a matter of concern until the mid–1970s.

Another factor that caused monetary authorities to take notice in the 1950s was the rise in velocity, the rate at which money is spent. During the contraction of the early 1930s, no one was surprised that velocity fell, because the public lost confidence in both the banking system and the economy. Therefore, the public wanted to hold more money as a percent of their income, a propensity that translates into a decrease in velocity. Economist John Maynard Keynes stated that "money lulls one's disquietude about the future." While velocity rose from 1932 to 1942, it began falling during World War II, reaching a low in 1946. This could have been the result of the rationing of consumer goods, or of the desire to evade taxes when engaging in black markets; we can only speculate on the reasons. Velocity rose after the war, especially after the Korean War began in June 1950. It fell briefly after pegging was stopped in 1951, because money was a safer asset than long-term government bonds, which were no longer "interest-bearing cash." From 1953 onward, velocity again rose as people held less money as a percent of their income. Some possible reasons were a more confident view of the future performance of the economy, higher interest rates on close money substitutes such as shares in savings and loan associations, and the possible belief that prices would rise, making money a less attractive asset.

As interest rates rose on short-term Treasury bills, corporations began acquiring them instead of holding idle demand deposits, on which no interest could be paid since 1933. Banks, as we shall see in the 1960s, had to become more aggressive in seeking deposits if they wanted large corporate deposits.

When velocity rises, the Fed has to take this into consideration when deciding how much to change the supply of money. For example, from the outbreak of the Korean War in June 1950 to February 1951, the increase in velocity was responsible for the 16 percent rise in wholesale prices because there was no increase in the money supply. But an increase in velocity can only carry the economy so far. In fact, this increase in wholesale prices was a strong motive for the Fed and the Treasury to agree to the accord, which caused a temporary decline in velocity as firms held more money and fewer long-term government bonds. But velocity resumed its upward movement in late 1954, and slowed only briefly in the recessions of 1958 and 1960.

Another problem facing the Fed in 1958 was the fact that prices rose rather than fell during the recession. This was something new, and various economists began offering their reasons for this surprising phenomenon. Some blamed strong unions for pushing their wages up above the market equilibrium level, causing business costs to rise, costs that were passed on in the form of higher prices but at a lesser level of output. Other economists, such as Abba Lerner and John Kenneth Galbraith, mentioned administered prices by large firms that had strong monopoly power, which prevented prices from falling when demand slackened. In both cases, less output would be produced, causing unemployment but with no appreciable decline in prices. Lerner and Galbraith, as well as others who gave these explanations for cost-push inflation, were usually pessimistic about the effectiveness of monetary policy. They argued that slowing the growth of the money supply to stop inflation from the cost side would make an already depressed economy suffer severe unemployment. They believed that large firms with monopoly power could pass the higher cost of credit on to their customers but the competitive sector, made up of small firms, would find credit unavailable. In addition, these economists pointed out that the large firms could even pass on the cost of a wage increase in the form of higher prices when that industry had excess capacity. Therefore, both Lerner and Galbraith advocated some form of price and wage controls for the sections of the economy that had this monopoly power.

Professor Sumner H. Slichter, while an opponent of price and wage controls, did believe that full employment and price stability were incompatible. He argued for a slow creep in the price level of perhaps

2 percent per year to keep the economy booming and prevent unnecessary unemployment. Even though he acknowledged that such an increase in the price level would erode life insurance, pension plans and savings in the long run, he felt this was the lesser of two evils. He also did not believe that a creeping inflation would turn into a serious one if the Fed kept the money supply growing at a moderate rate. Unfortunately as we shall see when looking at the 1970s, the Fed did not control the growth of the money supply very well. But one valuable suggestion Slichter made in the 1950s was the need for freer trade and allowing more foreign goods into the United States. This has reduced the ability of large firms to increase their prices when demand for their product has lessened.

Another economic study that was to affect the conduct of monetary policy for the next decade or so was one that related the change in wages (and also the price level) to the level of unemployment. The study was done by Professor A. W. Phillips in England, and this relationship when illustrated on a graph became known as the Phillips Curve. This study concluded that over the period from 1861 to 1913, when unemployment was low in Britain wages and prices rose, but when unemployment was high wages and prices were either stable or fell. This inverse relationship led many policy makers to feel there was a tradeoff between stable prices and full employment, and hence that the economy had to suffer a bit of inflation to keep workers fully employed. Paul Samuelson and his M.I.T. colleague Robert Solow published a very influential article in support of the existence of the tradeoff that the Phillips Curve indicated. They hinted that some form of wage and price intervention might be needed to improve this trade-off. This was to be especially important after the 1960 election when John Kennedy became President and surrounded himself with a Council of Economic Advisors who were disciples of Keynes and believed in this tradeoff. By the end of the 1960s, there were far fewer economists and policymakers who believed in the Phillips Curve.

The quantity theorists rejected the idea of a tradeoff between unemployment and inflation. These economists believed that if the Fed would hold the growth of money to a modest rate, any increases in wage rates or prices by monopoly firms above what the market would call for would result in unemployment and lost sales. Being rational, these decision makers would learn their lesson and moderate their behavior, rather than suffer loss of welfare. On the other hand, if the Fed ratified these wage or price increases, it would only encourage this aggressive type of action. One spokesman for the Fed during this time was Governor C. Canby Balderston, who as a professor of business had a good background in economics. He argued that monetary policy can keep inflation under control without causing too much unemployment.

As the decade of the 1950s came to an end, there was more discussion among academic economists about the relative merits of each of the Federal Reserve's operating tools. Most agreed that open market operations was the key tool, but there was disagreement about the others. Quantity theorists usually argued that the discount rate was no longer needed because banks could borrow needed reserves in the federal funds market from other banks at the going rate. To economists such as Milton Friedman, borrowing at the discount window was a subsidy to member banks. They also considered discounting to be a sanctioned source of slippage from a restrictive open market policy, slippage that would allow new reserves to leak back in when the Fed was trying to reduce them or to slow their growth through open market sales. The more liberal economists such as Paul Samuelson used the analogy that "good brakes make cars go faster." He meant that as long as the discount window is available as a safety value, the Fed could follow a tighter policy than normal, knowing that adversely affected banks could adjust their reserve positions by borrowing temporarily from the Fed.

However, the discount rate also has an announcement effect, which could reinforce Fed policy or act perversely. Unlike open market operations, which are carried on every day without the public being aware of them, a change in the discount rate makes news. It could signal the Fed is tightening or easing, but banks and business firms might respond opposite to the way the Fed would prefer. An increase in the rate might cause banks to borrow more from the Fed before rates go even higher. A decrease could cause banks to postpone borrowing in the hopes that rates would fall even more. But being a bureaucracy, the Fed would never voluntarily give up any tool or power even if it were considered archaic or perverse.

The newest tool, granted in 1935, was changing reserve requirements. Today this tool is rarely used, but it was the only tool the Fed could use when forced to peg the prices of government bonds. After the Korean War, the changes were almost always reductions, which pleased member banks. An increase in required reserves would cause banks to hold more non-interest-earning assets as a percent of total assets, so banks would never object to a reduction of their required reserves. Required reserves are the least liquid asset a bank holds because they cannot be used except at a penalty rate. Hence they function like a tax on member banks, which puts them at a disadvantage relative to non-member banks or other financial intermediaries. Higher reserve requirements, unless they are 100 percent, do not make a bank safer or more liquid.

One change in required reserves that occurred at the end of the 1950s was allowing member banks to count vault cash as part of their required reserves. From 1917 to 1959, only a member bank's deposit at its district Federal Reserve Bank could be counted as its legal reserve. But since all banks had to have vault cash to operate, this was an added expense to them because it was another non-interest-bearing asset that banks had to hold. Governor Balderston was the Fed's main proponent of making this change, which was clearly beneficial to member banks.

Selective controls, such as margin requirements on stock purchases and consumer and real estate credit, are direct interferences in a specific market. Margin requirements are still with us today, but the public seems to have adjusted to them. Consumer and real estate credit controls were allowed to lapse after the Korean War, but some Fed officials and Congressmen occasionally urge their reintroduction during inflationary times.

13

Operation Twist and President Kennedy's Tax Cut

The three recessions that occurred during the 1950s worked to the advantage of the incoming Kennedy administration because they seemed to rid the economy of inflationary expectations. This allowed an expansionary monetary and fiscal policy to have a greater impact on real output and less on prices, after the new president urged Congress "to get this country moving again." As an example, the narrow money supply, defined as currency and demand deposits, rose at an annual rate of 2.8 percent from 1951 through 1960, but this annual rate increased to 5.3 percent from 1961–1965. However, the average annual increase in the price level from the 1950s was 1.5 percent compared to only 1.3 percent from 1961 to 1965. The unemployment rate was a full point higher in the 1961–1965 period, 5.5 percent compared to 4.5 percent in the 1950s. The new president and his economic advisors, led by Walter Heller, were able to convince William McChesney Martin at the Fed to follow a more expansionary monetary policy by converting him to some Keynesian ideas. Two other well-known Keynesian economists, Gardner Ackley and James Tobin were also on President Kennedy's Council of Economic Advisors, While the money supply, as shown above, did increase at a faster rate in the Kennedy years, Martin still was less of an expansionist than the administration would have preferred. Martin did believe that fiscal policy had an important role to play and he agreed with Kennedy's voluntary wage and price guidelines, but opposed compulsory controls. He still used the analogy that the Fed's job was to "take away the punch bowl when the party was getting going."

The Kennedy administration was able to convince Martin to change from the "bills only" policy of open market operations, to one of "operation twist." The reason for this change was the fact that the U.S. was faced with two problems in the early 1960s: a balance of payments deficit, which caused a loss of gold; and a recession with too much unemployment. This new policy was designed to raise short-term interest rates while simultaneously lowering long-term rates.

The purpose of this plan was to encourage foreign holders of American short term securities to keep them invested in the New York money market, and not convert them to gold. That would hopefully stem the run on American gold. The other purpose of Operation Twist was to lower long-term interest rates to make business investment more profitable, and hence expand income and employment. The Fed was encouraged to sell large amounts of Treasury bills and simultaneously buy long-term government bonds. In this way, the large amount of short-term securities on the market would cause their price to fall, which would make their yields rise.

Conversely, the Fed's buying long-term bonds would drive up their price, causing their yields to fall. Private securities would be influenced by the prices of Treasury securities, because they are substitutes for one another. But government bond dealers were not pleased with this change because they had adjusted well to the "bills only" policy wherein rates were more predictable, causing fewer risks of loss. Only Governor James Robertson opposed ending the "bills only" policy, because he felt an increase in short-term interest rates would be harmful to the economy.

A major fiscal policy measure that Kennedy proposed was a large cut in income taxes. This took some selling on the part of Walter Heller of the Council of Economic Advisors. Many Congressmen, particularly Wilber Mills who was chairman of the House Ways and Means Committee, argued that there were no taxes to cut because the government's budget was in deficit. Heller introduced the public to the concept of the "Full Employment Surplus" which meant that the current rate of government spending and tax rates would result in a large surplus if the economy were at full employment. But the economy was not at full employment. Therefore, when the economy is operating in a recession, a deficit occurs because tax revenues fall and government transfer payments rise. Unemployed people do not pay taxes and do receive unemployment benefits from the federal government. Heller went on to argue that high tax rates prevent the economy from reaching full employment because they discourage spending.

So he proposed reducing income tax rates, which were at 20 percent at the lowest level and 91 percent at the highest level, to 14 percent and 70 percent respectively. One of President Kennedy's unofficial advisors, John Kenneth Galbraith, opposed cutting taxes. Instead, he wanted government spending to increase because he believed the public sector should provide more goods and services, while a tax cut would encourage more spending for private goods. Kennedy rejected this idea, preferring Heller's view. This debate continued and eventually Heller did convince Congress to enact the lower tax rates, but not until after Kennedy was assassinated and Johnson was president.

Another fiscal measure taken by Congress at President Kennedy's urging was an investment tax credit of 7 percent. This was passed in 1962 and allowed business firms to deduct 7 percent from their taxes when undertaking investment in new capital. This move was very popular with the business sector, and investment did increase. The Fed under Martin had slowed somewhat the growth rate of the money supply in early 1962 but increased this growth rate later that same year, which caused the economy to expand in 1963. Economists differed on whether this expansion was because of the investment tax credit or because of a more expansionary monetary policy.

A few years later, Walter Heller and Milton Friedman debated the impact of fiscal policy changes on the economy compared to the impact of monetary policy changes. Friedman argued that a change in fiscal policy alone, such as a tax cut or increased government spending without any expansion in the money supply, would merely crowd out a like amount of private spending, and thus be unable to increase income. Heller, while not denying that an expansion in fiscal policy would be more powerful if accompanied by an increase in the money supply, still believed that an increase in the government deficit, by either a tax cut or more government spending, would allow overall income to expand because the velocity of circulation would increase. The velocity increase, caused by higher interest rates making it more expensive to hold money balances idle, could come either from the government or from private firms spending money that otherwise would be held idle.

In early 1962, President Kennedy urged the private sector to follow his voluntary wage and price guidelines. The purpose was to prevent price increases by firms with monopoly power and wage increases by large unions that exceeded the rate of growth of real output. Economists Abba Lerner and John Kenneth Galbraith wanted compulsory price controls because they believed that "jawboning" or pleading for voluntary price restraint would not work. One incident that attracted national attention concerned wage negotiations in the steel industry in 1962. Kennedy used his influence with the steel union leaders, who had supported him in the 1960 election, to accept a modest wage increase as a patriotic move to keep down rising labor costs. The idea was that the steel companies would then hold down the price of their product, which was an important input into many other industries. When U.S. Steel announced a price increase after the labor settlement, Kennedy used the bully pulpit of the presidency to browbeat the president of U.S. Steel to rescind the price increase, much to the consternation of the business community. Many felt that these "voluntary" wage and price guidelines were a prelude to compulsory controls, which indeed came into being in 1971. In 1963, some small steel companies raised their prices and U.S. Steel "reluctantly" followed suit, giving credence to the view that voluntary price controls are ineffective.

Both Operation Twist and the wage and price guidelines were soon to disappear as inflation heated up in the mid–1960s with the Vietnam war and President Johnson's large increase in domestic spending for his "great society" programs. Inflation was to be the nation's most serious economic problem from the mid–1960s to the early 1980s.

14

Chairman Martin's Battle with President Johnson over Inflation

It took the assassination of President Kennedy and the ability of President Lyndon Johnson to persuade Congress to pass a large tax cut in April 1964. The economy expanded and unemployment fell by 1965. This seemed to verify the effectiveness of fiscal policy to overcome unemployment. The Keynesian school of economists were satisfied that they had finally been able to put their theories to work. However, the Fed under Martin also followed an expansionary monetary policy, so it was not obvious which of the two tools was the stronger. In any case, the optimism that followed the enactment of the tax cut did not last long.

The Vietnam War was taking more of the government's resources at the same time that President Johnson wanted to follow an expansionary domestic spending program, which he called "the war on poverty." Normally when a nation goes to war, taxes are increased and domestic programs are put aside. But this was not to be Johnson's plan. He argued that the nation could do both: fight a war in Southeast Asia and pursue large domestic spending programs at home. His economic advisors, mostly holdovers from the Kennedy administration, told him that a tax increase might be necessary. But it had taken over two years to convince Congress to cut taxes, so it would be difficult to go back and tell the public that taxes now had to be raised.

Chairman Martin and President Johnson had a major disagreement on how monetary policy should be conducted. Johnson wanted the Fed to follow an easy money policy so it could supply the bank reserves needed for the Treasury to sell its bonds without causing interest rates to rise. Martin was concerned about the inflationary impact of injecting new reserves into the banking system. As mentioned previously, when the Fed slows the growth of bank reserves with a tight money policy through open market operations, there is no announcement effect, so it normally takes a few months before the impact is felt throughout the economy. But an increase in the discount rate, while usually less effective, has an announcement effect immediately. In December 1965, the Fed raised the discount rate over Johnson's objections. Johnson even had Martin flown down to his Texas ranch for a barbeque and some browbeating, but Martin held his ground.

Other members of the Board of Governors supported Martin on this issue. James Robertson, a non-economist like Martin, had been reappointed to the board by Johnson in 1964 because he had been an easy money man up until that time. But in 1966, Robertson became known as a "pro-crunch" man who believed that tight money or the threat of it would stop inflation, even if it caused some banks and financial intermediaries to go bankrupt.

Sherman Maisel, an economist on the board, was well aware of the impact of high interest rates on the housing market and small businesses, but he too voted with Martin in late 1965 and early 1966. He supported the Fed's use of the threat of denial of discount window privileges to pressure banks to refrain from expanding their loans too rapidly. Maisel also supported the Fed's move to increase the maximum interest rates that banks could pay on various time deposits through its Regulation Q. This power was similarly extended to savings and loan associations and savings banks through their respective federal insurance agencies.

A new appointee to the Board of Governors also supported Martin's tight money policy, even though Martin had opposed this man's appointment to the board. The man was Andrew Brimmer, the first black person to serve on the board. Martin's objection was not because of race, but because Brimmer was an economist, and Martin felt the Board was becoming overly influenced by economists. As we will see later, the Board today consists almost entirely of economists, and a person with no economic training would feel out of place in that setting. Martin also opposed the 1970 appointment of his successor as chairman, Arthur Burns, because he too was an economist. Brimmer was appointed because Johnson thought he was an easy money man, but Brimmer disappointed him. The December discount rate increase moved the rate to the highest it had been since 1929, 4.50 percent, while the federal funds rate was 5.11 percent. Brimmer, who was told by Martin that he would be a junior appointee, did support these moves. But in late 1966, Brimmer argued for suspension of the 1962 investment tax credit and for an increase in income taxes.

With the expansion in bank reserves, and the depletion of the nation's gold stock because of the balance of payments deficit, the Fed was having difficulty maintaining the 25 percent reserve requirement in gold certificates for its liabilities in member bank reserves and federal reserve notes. So without much fanfare, Congress eliminated the 25 percent reserve requirement against the member bank reserves held at the Fed. For the next three years, the Fed's only reserve requirement was the 25 percent against its notes. When that became impossible to maintain in 1968, that too was eliminated by Congress, freeing the Fed completely from any gold reserve requirements. Those two reserve requirements had served as an anchor for the Fed and for Martin who believed in them. However, he was forced by circumstances to acquiesce in their removal. It took over 50 years from its inception, but what many economists knew from the beginning finally came to realization. A central bank and the gold standard are incompatible because the former relies on discretion, and the latter on automatic rules. Whenever the gold limits were reached, the gold reserve requirements were either suspended (1918 and 1933), reduced (1945), or abolished (1965 and 1968).

Even though President Johnson disagreed with Chairman Martin, he did reappoint Martin as chairman for his last four-year term in 1966. Public opinion may have played a role in this decision. The money crunch of 1966 was responsible for a new word in financial circles: "disintermediation." The public normally saves through financial intermediaries such as banks, savings and loan associations, savings banks and credit unions. These institutions pool the savings of many small savers, and lend large amounts to those who wish to borrow for homes or consumer durables. This reduces the risk to savers by spreading the risk of default over many borrowers. It makes it convenient for a borrower to acquire needed funds by going to a single institution, and not having to borrow small amounts from many different sources. But when market interest rates rise above the maximum interest rates that these institutions can pay because of Regulation Q, savers pull their money out of these financial intermediaries and invest directly in the financial market. In 1966, this bypassing of financial intermediaries is called "disintermediation." Savers could get a higher rate on Treasury bills or bonds of other federal agencies like the Federal National Mortgage Association, the Federal Land Banks, or the Federal Home Loan Banks. Many consumers also bought corporate bonds, which yielded higher interest rates than what Regulation Q allowed. To offset this, the Treasury stopped selling its ninety-day and six-month bills in $1000 units, and raised the minimum to $10,000. But this did not stop disintermediation because of the other alternatives.

The financial institution most adversely affected was the savings and loan association, which in turn hurt the housing sector severely. These institutions were strictly regulated by the federal government in order to subsidize the financing of homes. They could only invest in long-term mortgages but acquired their funds by offering the public share accounts, which were viewed by the public as a perfect substitute for passbook savings accounts at commercial banks. The Federal Savings and Loan Association insured these share accounts up to the same maximum as the FDIC used for bank accounts. But as we will see in the 1980s, this was not insurance but a federal guarantee that obligated the tax payers to pay what the insurance fund could not.

The laws then in place governing the way savings and loan associations could operate were bound to cause a severe problem. These single-purpose institutions were restricted to making home mortgages in an area close to where their office was located, but they acquired their funds by offering a share account that the public assumed it could cash in at any time. In effect, they were borrowing short and lending long. During the 1950s and early 1960s this did not seem to hurt them, because they received enough new money to meet the withdrawals. In fact, savings and loan associations in growing areas, such as California advertised nationwide for funds with the appeal that these funds were federally insured and paid a higher rate than alternatives. But with the increase in interest rates on Treasury bills and other alternatives in the mid–1960s, the public wanted to withdraw their savings from these institutions and invest in assets that paid higher interest rates. In 1966, the savings and loan associations had almost no money to lend but were faced with large withdrawals. In order to meet these withdrawals, they had to borrow from the Federal Home Loan Banks, which were established to help these institutions in financial distress. But the Federal Home Loan Banks could not create money as the Federal Reserve could, so they had to sell bonds in the capital market with their federal guarantee. These sales put more pressure on the capital market, causing long-term interest rates to rise.

By 1968, inflation was heating up. President Johnson got Congress to suspend the 7 percent investment tax credit and to pass his 10 percent surcharge on income taxes. The Fed, with Martin's approval, increased the money supply because of the fear of fiscal overkill. The tax surcharge did cause the federal budget to go into surplus in fiscal 1969, but the easy money policy allowed the price level to keep rising. Martin later admitted he had made a mistake in following an easy money policy, which left a legacy of the worst inflation the U.S. economy had experienced since the Civil War up until that time. This was Martin's own assessment of his actions.

Martin still believed the Fed should follow many goals. He felt the Fed should not consider only price stability but also the level of employment, balance of payments equilibrium, and the conditions of the government bond market. His instructions to the New York trading desk were always vague: *Continue a moderate restraint, or maintain the existing degree of restraint with lesser restraint possible if conditions warrant it.* He testified before Congress that he was concerned with the "tone" and "feel" of the government bond market. These terms frustrated members of Congress, causing Senator Proxmire to remark that trying to pin Martin down was like trying to nail a custard pie to the wall. What bothered critics, especially academic critics, was that the manager of the New York trading desk was allowed to attend the meetings of the FOMC and listen to all the various discussions. If he were not present, the directions to him would have to be more specific.

As more Kennedy and Johnson appointees were put on the Board of Governors, Martin was getting fewer unanimous votes, but Martin was usually with the majority although he had acquired some enemies in Congress during the 1960s. Both Senator Russell Long and Congressman Wright Patman opposed his reappointment by President Johnson in 1966. As mentioned previously, Martin resented the appointment of so many economists to the Board of Governors. President Johnson appointed Sherman Maisel, an economist from the University of California, to the board in 1965, followed by William Sherrill, who had an excellent background in finance, in 1967. These appointees joined Dewey Daane and Andrew Brimmer, economists already on the board.

Other measures taken by the Fed in the late 1960s concerned interest rate ceilings. Some board members such as Andrew Brimmer wanted to abolish Regulation Q and let banks and other deposit-type institutions pay market rates on all accounts. Instead, Congress passed the Interest Rate Adjustment Act that allowed higher rates to be paid on certificates of deposit over $100,000 and lower rates for those below that amount. Thus, businesses and wealthy individuals could get market rates on their savings but the ordinary person could not. Interest ceilings were extended to thrift institutions (savings and loan associations, savings banks and credit unions) but the latter were allowed to pay a slightly higher rate than commercial banks.

In 1968, with the Fed's easy money policy, the national income rose 10 percent and unemployment fell to 3.8 percent of the work force, a rate than had not been seen since the Korean War. One explanation for the low unemployment may have been the workings of the Phillips Curve tradeoff between inflation and unemployment. But the Phillips Curve describes a shortrun situation wherein workers are fooled into agreeing to a wage that would be acceptable if prices were stable, but is not acceptable when the price level rises because this reduces workers' purchasing power. Prior to 1965 the U.S. had not experienced much inflation, so large labor unions exchanged their cost-of-living escalator clauses for other considerations in their wage contracts, because the unions did not expect inflation. But once those contracts came up for renewal, unions wanted the cost-of-living clauses reinserted. After that was back in the contract, inflation could no longer reduce the rate of unemployment, as the economy sadly experienced in the dismal 1970s. So belief in the Phillips Curve tradeoff was shattered.

One change that William McChesney Martin wanted to make, but that still has not been implemented, would be to make the four-year term of the chairman of the Board of Governors coincide with the term of the President. In 1969, President Nixon came into office and had to deal with Martin for a full year before putting his own choice, Arthur Burns, in that position. The same thing was to occur in 1977 when President Carter had to deal with Burns for a full year when he wanted to make a change. But the 1935 Amendment to the Federal Reserve Act had been designed to make the Fed independent of both the president and Congress. Making the chairman's term coincide with that of the president would reduce that independence.

15

Nixon Replaces Martin with Burns and Inflicts Price Controls on the Economy

In 1969 the Fed followed a tight money policy, which caused the money supply to increase by only 1.5 percent on an annual basis. The discount rate was increased to its highest level in 40 years. With Regulation Q preventing banks from paying market rates on their sources of funds, banks resorted to alternative sources of funds not subject to interest rate ceilings. These included federal funds, in which large banks in money centers could acquire reserves from banks in areas where loan demand was not as strong. Banks also were able to raise funds through the sale of commercial paper by their holding company affiliate. This involved borrowing Eurodollars from foreign affiliates and selling debentures, which were unsecured, non-deposit liabilities of the bank. Large firms also began bypassing banks as sources of funds by selling securities in the capital and money markets. In 1970, Congress gave the Fed the power to regulate the one-bank holding companies, which were designed to evade Regulation Q.

President Nixon wanted to appoint economist Arthur Burns as Chairman of the Board of Governors as soon as possible. Burns, a respected economist and president of the National Bureau of Economic Research, had been chairman of President Eisenhower's Council of Economic Advisors during 1953–1957. In 1969, Nixon made Burns head of Nixon's policy development, a "position in waiting" for Martin's term to end. Nixon had not forgotten Martin's tight money policy in 1959 and 1960 that had caused a recession, which Nixon felt had cost him the 1960 election. Martin's term as chairman was to expire on January 31, 1970, and both Nixon and Burns felt Martin would stay in that position until midnight Hawaii time. The dismal decade of the 1970s was beginning, but at the time no one could foresee that events were to make it second only to the 1930s as the worst economic experience of the twentieth century.

Martin's reputation for hard money and stable prices was ruined by the last two or three years of his term. One of the economists on the Board of Governors, Sherman Maisel, said that Martin was mostly on the side of expansion in the 1960s and overly concerned with the condition of financial markets. While Martin did establish the Fed's independence from the Treasury, he left his position at a time of recession and inflation. But it was in 1970, Martin's last year on the Board, that the Fed, with Sherman Maisel's influence, began putting more emphasis on the supply of money as a guide for monetary policy decisions than on interest rates.

In the 1960s, the Fed often used "free reserves" or "net borrowed reserves" as a guide to open market operations. Free reserves were excess reserves minus those reserves that came from member bank borrowing at the Fed. Net borrowed reserves was the term used if free reserves were negative. Originally, the Fed assumed that banks may be reluctant to borrow from their district Federal Reserve Bank, so reserves from that source may be temporary and not used for expanding loans. But this thinking proved to be incorrect in the late 1960s and early 1970s because of the inflationary expectations. It was soon discovered that a constant level of free reserves did not mean that monetary policy was unchanged.

This was especially the case when the Fed's defensive operations were taken into account. Defensive operations are open market operations designed to offset unwanted changes in the money supply. For example, if the public wants to use more currency, or the if Treasury transfers funds from its accounts in commercial banks to its account at the Federal Reserve, this causes bank reserves to go down, so the Fed buys more bonds to keep reserves the same. These defensive operations actually account for many times the open market operations that the Fed undertakes specifically to change bank reserves to the desired level. With banks often borrowing needed reserves from the Fed during periods of defensive operations, it makes the level of free reserves even more unpredictable. In fact, Chairman Martin was quoted as saying he rued the day he first heard of free reserves.

Another change in Fed policy in the last two years of Martin's tenure as chairman was the adoption of lagged reserve accounting, as opposed to contemporaneous reserve accounting. Lagged reserve accounting meant that member banks were to count their reserve requirements on the deposits of two weeks earlier, rather than on deposits of the current week. But to complicate matters, the vault cash of the current week was counted as part of the required reserves that banks had to meet at the close of business every Wednesday. This change made it more difficult for the Fed to control the money supply and therefore was widely criticized by economists, but it remained in effect until 1984.

Another change that helped consumers was the Fed's implementation of the rules for a law passed by Congress in 1968, the Truth-in-Lending Law. This meant that banks and other financial institutions had to disclose the actual rate of interest that a consumer would pay on an annual basis on each loan transaction. Two non-economists on the Board of Governors, lawyers James Robertson and Jeffrey Bucher, were instrumental in following up on this legislation. Robertson had been on the board since 1952, which was before economists came to dominate board positions. But when Bucher was appointed in 1972, he had to undergo hostile questions at his confirmation hearing from Senator Proxmire, who believed that only economists should be in these positions. Bucher, who had been with a California bank, was not even considered a "real" banker because he had been with the trust department, which is not a main function of commercial banking. Nevertheless, Bucher was confirmed and, at age 39, was the youngest governor to serve on the board up until then. He took the lead in writing consumer legislation that made lenders reveal the actual rate of interest that consumers had to pay.

The first year of Burns' term on the board was one of mild recession but also of inflation. Even though Burns tried a gradual slowing of the money growth, the money supply (defined as currency and checkable deposits) rose at 5.5 percent in 1970. The recession was over by the end of 1970, but the money growth rate remained fairly high because Burns felt that the need for liquidity outweighed the case for the tight money policy needed to fight inflation. This was especially so after the failure of Penn Central Railroad to meet its obligations when its commercial paper came due. The Fed announced that its discount window would be open, which allowed new reserves to enter the banking system. In addition, the Fed increased the interest ceiling banks could pay on large certificates of deposit, so that banks would not lose those corporate deposits to the money market.

In August 1971, Burns backed President Nixon's imposition of price and wage controls. Burns had always been opposed to controls, but he supported Nixon because he felt that the economy was not working the way it once had. Inflation did not come down fast enough to suit the electorate, and after the Republicans lost seats in the 1970 elections, the urge to do something outweighed economic reasoning. Congress had given Nixon the power to control wages and prices in the Economic Stabilization Act of 1970. At the time, Nixon said he did not want this power. Burns felt that collective bargaining agreements were not responding to anti-inflationary policy, and that some type of "incomes policy" was needed. Initially, there was a ninety-day freeze on wages and prices, which was followed by three other phases that gradually loosened the controls. All controls were eliminated by April 1974.

Most academic economists were appalled by these controls, especially those economists who were advocates of free market policies. But Nixon's popularity rose after the controls were installed, because many people felt that this was an attempt to really do something to control inflation. Controls had been used in World War II, but the Vietnam War, which was still being waged, was not a total war as in the 1940s. While the controls were in place, the money supply in 1971 grew at 6.6 percent but increased to 7.9 percent in 1972, which was an election year. Critics of the Fed accused Burns of increasing the growth of the money supply to re-elect Nixon, but Burns denied this. If the money supply increases during normal times, it can impact both prices and output if the economy is at less than full employment. However, if prices are frozen, then the increase in the money supply will primarily impact output when the economy has unused resources, which could lead to more employment temporarily.

When Senator Proxmire in 1973 questioned Burns' policies, Burns admitted that the increase in the money supply was perhaps a bit high. But Burns blamed the inflation on non-monetary factors such as crop failures, oil embargoes, and shortages of critical materials, as well as depreciation of the dollar in foreign markets, making it more expensive for Americans to import from abroad. Part of Nixon's new economic policy was to close the gold window and allow the price of gold and the foreign exchange value of the American dollar to fluctuate freely in the world market. Prior to this, the price of gold had been raised to $42 per ounce, but this was only a stop gap measure. The value of the American dollar fell compared to most other countries' currencies, making it easier for American firms to sell abroad. While ending the fixed exchange rate of the Bretton Woods system that had been in effect since the end of World War II was a desirable thing because it was impossible for the Americans to maintain the dollar at even the $42 an ounce price, the price and wage controls were a disaster. They caused shortages and misallocation of resources. The country experienced long lines at gasoline stations as well as other critical shortages. In addition, while crop failures and oil embargoes can cause certain prices to rise, they reflect changes in relative prices and are not the cause of overall inflation. What is confusing to the public is that oil and food are put in the consumer price index. Therefore, when they rise in price, that index must also rise, but that is not a correct measure of inflation. While there is no perfect measure of inflation, economists of the quantity theory school argued that it was the increase in the rate of growth of the money supply that caused the inflation.

16

Supply Shocks in the 1970s Make Unemployment and Inflation Worse

The economy suffered both rising prices and more unemployment as the controls came off in 1973 and 1974. Sellers began raising prices as the controls were lifted, but the economy was hit by some supply shocks that caused output to fall while prices were rising. A new term, "stagflation," was used to describe an economy suffering simultaneously from these two evils. Politicians who were out of office devised a "misery index," which added the unemployment rate to the inflation rate, to attack the party in office. The economy went into a severe recession from late 1973 to the first quarter of 1975. The price level rose at 12.2 percent in 1974, and hit 14 percent at the peak. Unemployment reached 9 percent, and with rising prices, the unemployed were in worse shape than in previous recessions.

One of the distressing factors of the 1973–1975 recession was the way the cost-of-living escalator clauses worked in some labor contracts, particularly in the auto industry. When the price level rose because of higher oil prices after the OPEC embargo, auto firms were obligated to pay higher wages to their workers because the consumer price index rose. But the demand for American cars fell, because the public shifted its demand to foreign cars that got better mileage. Large layoffs occurred, but the remaining workers did receive these cost-of-living increases.

This recession was now the worst the American economy had experienced since World War II, surpassing even the 1957–1958 downturn. There were large decreases in inventories; industrial production dropped about 15 percent. In July 1974, Gerald Ford became president when Nixon resigned, and immediately signaled that the main danger to the economy was inflation. He wore a WIN button to a news conference, stating that the letters stood for Whip Inflation Now. Arthur Burns and the other board members wanted to follow a tight money policy. But the failure of the Franklin National Bank in the fall of 1974 caused the Fed to open the discount window to prevent panic, just as it had when the Penn Central failed in 1970. So this worked to offset a restrictive open market policy. One of the newer governors on the board, Robert C. Holland, was an economist who had held various research positions with the Fed since 1961. He was influential in getting the FOMC to concentrate on monetary aggregates (reserves for private deposits) and put less emphasis on interest rates as a guide to controlling the money supply. Before Holland left the board in May 1976, the consumer price index did slow down from increasing at a rate of over 12 percent in 1974 to just 4.9 percent per year. However, unemployment was higher than normal.

One change that the Ford administration made was the repeal of the prohibition against American citizens holding gold, which the Roosevelt administration had imposed in 1933. In 1975, gold had been completely divorced from any impact on the money supply, so the American public was now allowed to acquire gold for any purpose they wanted. When inflation became severe in early 1980, gold traded at over $800 an ounce. The public obviously felt it was a good hedge against inflation.

Economists often speak of a natural rate of unemployment, which is the level of unemployment a market economy moves toward when it is experiencing neither inflation nor deflation. During the 1950s, most economists believed that 4 percent unemployment represented "full employment," which meant that it would not be possible to get below that figure without causing unexpected inflation. This rate of unemployment coincided with the normal changes in a free labor market where some workers are between jobs and others just entering the labor force. But in comparing the 1950s to the 1970s, labor economists pointed out two structural changes. Teenagers and women had higher unemployment rates than adult men, and in the 1930s the birth rate had been low, so there were fewer teenagers to affect the 1950s unemployment rate. Moreover, in the 1950s not as many women entered the labor force as in the 1970s. Since the 1950s was part of the baby boom, it created a lot teenagers for the labor force in the 1970s. In addition, the increased cost of living from the higher inflation may have caused more housewives to enter the job market. So the natural rate of unemployment was raised from 4 percent to 5.5 percent. Politicians, however, would try to make this higher rate of unemployment a campaign issue.

One of the unfortunate things about stagflation is that there is no macro-type policy that the Fed or Congress can follow to improve the situation. If they concentrate on inflation, they can make unemployment worse with a restrictive monetary policy, as President Ford wanted to do with his WIN policy. If they focus on unemployment, an expansionary monetary policy can cause inflation to accelerate without improving the unemployment. So academic economists would give policymakers the hardest instructions any politician would ever have to follow: Do nothing! But with the public clamoring for relief, the urge for the government to do something was irresistible.

While the Fed is supposed to be independent of both the president and Congress, it is very difficult for the FOMC to ignore the pleas for easy money. During the restrictive money crunches of 1966 and 1969, the Fed eased up before they were able to rid the economy of inflationary expectations. For most of the 1970s, expansionary policies were pushed too far. During inflation, nominal interest rates rise, and policymakers can mistakenly believe that high interest rates are going to depress investment. But investment depends on expected real interest rates, which are the nominal rates minus the rate of inflation. So in some years of the 1970s, real rates were negative when the rate of inflation was higher than the interest rate. These high nominal rates caused velocity to rise as the public wanted to keep its cash balances as low as possible. As the public wanted to hold very little in non-interest deposits, banks wanted to hold very little in non-interest reserves.

It was in the climate of the inflationary 1970s that the distinction between what was money and what was not money became clouded. Before then, people could spend only coins, and currency or write checks on their demand deposits, which only commercial banks could issue. Other near monies, such as savings accounts in banks and share accounts in savings and loan associations or credit unions, had to be cashed in for currency or transferred to a checking account before they could be spent. But around 1972, some mutual savings banks in New England began offering negotiated order of withdrawals, or NOW accounts. It started very simply. Depositors could use these NOW accounts only to pay utility bills. Instead of going to the savings bank and withdrawing currency, the depositor could send the check-like instrument to the utility company, who would accept it for payment and forward it to the commercial bank where the savings bank kept its checking account. After the commercial bank reduced the savings bank's account, it would send the NOW receipt to the savings bank who would reduce the depositor's savings account. This is shown below:

Commercial Bank		Savings Bank	
Assets	*Liabilities*	*Assets*	*Liabilities*
	+Util Acct	– Acct at Bank	– NOW Acct
	-Sav. Bank Acct		of customer

It was not very long before these NOW accounts could be used as regular checking accounts for any purpose, and not too long before commercial banks began offering similar products, such as sweep accounts. The latter would allow a bank customer to keep all his money in a savings account and have a zero balance in his checking account. As checks were written on the zero balance account, the money was swept by the bank from the interest-bearing savings account into the checking account to cover the amount of the check. This was a way to pay interest on checking accounts that the 1933 law forbad.

Another substitute for a bank's checking account was the money market mutual fund. Mutual funds that heretofore had gathered funds from savers and pooled them to buy stocks or bonds now offered high market interest rates on funds that worked like a checking account. The funds pooled were used to buy Treasury bills, commercial paper, or other safe short-term money market instruments that paid higher interest rates than Regulation Q allowed banks to pay. The consumer could use a checklike instrument to pay for items and the seller would send it to his bank, which in turn would send it to the bank where the money market fund did its banking. The fund's checking balance would be reduced; would reduce the amount of shares the consumer owned, and would sell some of its Treasury bills or other market instruments it had been holding. These funds made velocity rise and made it more difficult for the Fed to control spending by controlling bank reserves. With interest rates higher than Regulation Q ceilings, these money market mutual funds rose in volume from $3.3 billion in 1977 to $186.9 billion in 1981.

17

Carter Replaces Burns with Miller and Inflation Worsens

The first year of the Carter administration was in one respect similar to the first year of the Nixon administration in 1969. In each case, the new president was saddled with an unwanted chairman of the Board of Governors of the Federal Reserve. Chairman Burns opposed Carter's proposal to give everyone a $50 tax rebate in 1977. So at the end of January 1978, Carter replaced Burns with G. William Miller, whose only connection with the Fed or monetary policy was as a director of the Federal Reserve Bank of Boston. Miller had graduated from the U.S. Coast Guard Academy, and after his active duty went to law school at the University of California, Berkeley, where he graduated at the top of his class. He was very successful in the business world, becoming chief executive officer at Textron. He took a pay cut from $380,000 per year to $57,500 as Fed chairman.

But Miller was not the man for this job. At the Senate hearings, Senator Proxmire pointed out Miller's lack of economic training. Miller responded that he could fight inflation and unemployment at the same time, but he did not state how. He seemed to feel that fighting inflation was outside the Fed's control because it required lower deficits, lower energy costs, and more capital investment. His confirmation hearing took five weeks, but not because of his evasive answers to those questioning his background, such as his statement that his goal was to become "rookie of the year." Rather, the long period of questioning got sidetracked on his business ethics when the committee asked about a payment from one of Textron's subsidiaries to a sales representative from Iran. Miller was able to defend himself from any unethical behavior, and only Proxmire voted against his confirmation because of his lack of economic background.

Miller had been critical of Burns' policy as being too tight, so it was no surprise that Miller wanted an easy money policy. He believed that a restrictive monetary policy would lead to serious market disruptions. He said that inflation was not a result of an easy money policy but of rising labor costs, farm price supports, higher employer costs for social security, import restrictions, and the general inflationary psychology. Most economists would argue that these factors are the result of inflation and not its cause, which would be a growth of the money supply in excess of the growth of output.

As inflation accelerated throughout 1978, Miller still argued that a restrictive monetary policy would have great social costs. He stated that he wanted to run the Fed for human beings and not use monetary policy to create a recession. But human beings also suffer in inflationary times. The price level rose 13 percent in 1979 after rising 9 percent in 1978. In addition, oil prices rose 87 percent, the functional equivalent of an excise tax on the public.

Miller encountered opposition on the board and from members of the FOMC on his management style. Scholarly debates were discouraged; a swift decision was his goal. Miller was accustomed to corporate board meetings, but not to academic discussions among economists. He cut weekly meetings of the board from three to two. He began to be outvoted when the discount rate was increased from 7.00 percent to 7.25 percent in October 1978 and again when it was increased to 8.25 percent in November. The latter increase was announced by Secretary of the Treasury, Michael Blumenthal, and not by Miller, which was very unusual.

Miller also annoyed Congress when he wanted to pay interest to member banks on their reserve deposits at their district Federal Reserve Banks. Miller was concerned about the large number of banks withdrawing from the Federal Reserve system in order to get lower reserve requirements that some states allow. Congress turned down this proposal, because the Fed turns most of its interest income on government bonds over to the Treasury, which reduces the interest cost of the federal debt. Even though many economists had actually advocated Miller's suggestion in the past, Miller unfortunately wanted to bypass Congress on this and change the rule himself. He was unable to accomplish this, and made some enemies in the process.

By the summer of 1979, the need to curb inflation was evident. The demand for credit was increasing sharply even in the face of higher nominal interest rates, because inflationary expectations led borrowers to expect even higher rates in the future. Gold, which had been pegged at $35 an ounce ten years before, now sold for $500 per ounce. The consumer price index had risen 35 percent and the broader price measure, the GNP deflator, had risen 30 percent between 1975 and 1979. The narrow money supply (currency and demand deposits) had risen 32 percent, and velocity increased 18 percent over that same four-year period. President Carter knew it was time for a change.

Miller was being outvoted in the FOMC meetings concerning the conduct of open market operations. One person who was sympathetic to his views was Nancy Teeters the first woman on the board. When Carter replaced Burns with Miller, Burns still had six years to go on his term on the board, but unlike Marriner Stoddard Eccles, Burns would not stay on the Board when he was no longer chairman. So Carter got a second appointment, Teeters, who was trained as an economist, but who also believed that tight money hurts certain sectors of the economy such as housing and small business. However, some others on the board, such as Henry Wallich, were strong anti-inflation hawks. Wallich had experienced the German hyperinflation of the early 1920s as a child and knew of its devastation. At first he was the lone dissenter at some of the early FOMC meetings under Miller, but he was becoming more persuasive. In July 1979, Carter fired four cabinet members including Michael Blumenthal, and asked Miller to become his Secretary of the Treasury. Miller accepted, although technically he could have stayed at the Fed even if Carter no longer wanted him there. Governors on the board cannot be removed until their term is up. But it seemed Miller was happy to go to the Treasury where there would be fewer academic-type debates on policy.

Governors such as Miller and Teeters, who fear the use of a restrictive monetary policy because it adversely affects certain sectors, often downplay the damage that inflation can do. Some easy money people believe that a perfectly anticipated inflation would not do much harm, because borrowers and lenders and other decision makers would take the inflation rate into account when entering contracts. But no one predicted the sharp rate of inflation that occurred in the 1970s when the consumer price index more than doubled, from 38.8 to 82.4. This was a scale that used 1983 as the base year, or a price level of 100. Such a decade made a mockery of one who was thrifty and saved for the future.

Inflation also has adverse effects on capital formation. The rate of inflation can not only distort real interest rates by unpredictable rises in prices, but also can cause firms to misjudge future consumer demand and invest in unprofitable areas. Once this occurs, this capital will fall in value and depreciation will be insufficient to replace it. Inflation also causes saving to decline. Individuals have to increase their consumption and reduce their saving if they want to maintain their normal standard of living. Progressive income taxes divert funds from those most likely to save to those at the lower portion of the income scale who will spend most of their income. Saving declined in real terms (corrected for inflation) from $158.7 billion in 1975 to $100 billion in 1981.

A further factor discouraging investment is that our tax laws are based on nominal, not real, income. Firms are, in effect, made to pay taxes based on imaginary and not real earnings, especially when they cannot take the real depreciation charges needed to replace their capital, because replacement cost has risen. The same applies to those individuals who move into higher tax brackets. They are often taxed on illusionary capital gains and are forced to pay a higher percentage of their income in taxes when their real income has not increased. When faced with sharp inflation, individuals begin to allocate their savings to non-money items such as gold, land, art work, or other assets that they hope will rise in value faster than the price level. This requires major corrections that would not be necessary if the price level were stable and the public were satisfied with normal savings accounts or bonds.

Even if the government indexes the federal income tax or social security payments to the price level, this occurs after the fact, as real income is lost. In addition, it is only partial indexing. Capital gains, corporate depreciation, and personal interest or rental income are not included. It would be better to get rid of inflation than to try to eliminate its harmful effects through indexation.

In the business world, inflation makes a hero out of the financial officer who can predict changes in interest rates correctly, and who can minimize a firm's cash balances and keep the company funds invested in short-term securities at the highest rates. The production manager who can increase output per man-hour or the product designer who can come up with an improved product often takes a back seat to the financial wizard. In normal times, these latter two would be the key people in a firm, but inflation makes the "Fed watcher," the person who can take advantage of changes in government policy, the most important one in the firm. But as classical economists of old taught us, the way to increase real wealth is to produce goods and services that increase the welfare of the economy. Outguessing inflation in the 1970s could make a particular firm or individual wealthy, but not the community at large. Looking back at that unfortunate decade, we find the worst inflation years were 1973 (8.8%), 1974 (12.2%), 1978 (9%), and 1979 (13.3%). On the other hand, the worst years for unemployment were 1975 (8.5%), 1976 (7.7%) and 1978 (6.1%).

18

The Volcker Era Begins and the Fed Gets Control Over All Banks

Paul Volcker was not President Carter's first choice for Chairman of the Board of Governors to replace G. William Miller. Carter first offered the job to David Rockefeller, an economist and president of Chase Manhattan Bank, and then to A. W. Clausen, president of the Bank of America, but both turned him down. Volcker had been on the FOMC since 1975 when he replaced Alfred Hayes as president of the New York Federal Reserve Bank. In that position, he usually voted with Henry Wallich as one of the anti-inflation hawks in opposition to Miller and Teeters, the doves. Several of Carter's advisors were against Volcker's appointment because they believed his strong anti-inflation stance would hurt Carter's reelection chances in 1980, which is exactly what happened.

Volcker was an economist with a great deal of experience in the international field even though he never completed his Ph.D. dissertation. As Under Secretary of the Treasury in the Nixon administration, he worked with the International Monetary Fund, trying to make the fixed exchange system work, it being the system he preferred. But when it broke down in 1971, he accepted the floating rate system because he realized that under the fixed rate system, all the pressure to restore equilibrium was put on the deficit country. Volcker spent one year at his alma mater, Princeton University, during the Fall of 1974 and the spring of 1975, a year that helped him develop his own brand of monetarism. He admired the contributions of the monetarists such as distinguishing between real and nominal interest rates. Monetarist's also pointed out the lags between the time of taking policy action and the time of its impact on the economy, and thus the futility of the kind of "fine tuning" that the Keynesian economists usually advocated. Volcker also liked the idea of Congress mandating that the Fed announce its monetary targets, but without specifying which measure of money should be used. But Volcker did not accept the monetarists' constant-growth-of-money rule because he believed that the money supply was not the only factor that impacted the health of the economy.

In moving from the presidency of the New York Fed to the chairmanship of the Board of Governors, Volcker took a pay cut from $116,000 to $57,500, which was a great financial sacrifice since his wife elected to stay in New York because she was undergoing treatment with a particular doctor. It was said he lived like a poor graduate student in a tiny Washington apartment. But taking over the leadership of the Fed at this crucial time was an opportunity to do something about the chronic inflation that was in double digits. When asked by a reporter if we were gong to have a recession, Volcker gave an astounding answer for a public official: "Yes, and the sooner the better."

It was Volcker's belief that inflation had to come down quickly even if it did cause a serious recession. He argued against the monetarist position favoring a slower decline in the rate of growth of the money supply, because he felt the public would not go along with a slow reduction. Using his experience in the real world, Vockler made the point that some crisis usually comes up that puts political pressure on the Fed to ease up, a crisis such as the failure of a large bank or some international disturbance. Tight money in 1966, 1969 and 1975 did not last long enough to break the inflationary expectations. The failures of the Penn Central Railroad in 1970 and the Franklin National Bank in 1974 were examples Volcker used. In each case, the Fed was subjected to great pressure to ease up and it did.

Shortly after taking the reins as chairman, Volcker met with the new Secretary of the Treasury, G. William Miller, his predecessor at the Fed, along with officials of both West Germany and the International Monetary Fund in Hamburg, Germany. The point was made that the U.S. had to control its inflation because the Europeans would no longer support the dollar. Volcker hurried home and called a special meeting of the FOMC on Saturday, October 6, 1979, at which meeting it was decided to break the public's expectations of inflation. The discount rate was raised from 11 percent to 12 percent, and an 8 percent reserve requirement was placed on managed bank liabilities that were used to evade reserves on deposits. These included debentures, Eurodollars, and the use of commercial paper by the one-bank holding companies. But most importantly, the Fed announced it would conduct its open market operations by concentrating on non-borrowed reserves, and let the federal funds rate fluctuate freely. It was the view of both Volcker and Wallich that targeting reserves would face less opposition than targeting the federal funds rate, because the public could see that market forces and not the Fed caused interest rates to increase. However, the Fed did not completely abandon using the federal funds rate; the Fed actually allowed the rate to fluctuate within a wider range than previously.

From late October 1979 until March 1980 the money supply slowed, but the sharp increase in interest rates annoyed President Carter. The president invoked the 1969 Credit Control Act to force the Fed to implement special measures of credit restraint. Volcker disliked these measures, which he considered an interference with specific markets, but he had to go along with them. Volcker supported that part of the Humphrey-Hawkins Act of 1978 that required the Fed to tell Congress what its growth rates of money were for that year. His October 1979 meeting of the FOMC was meant to emphasize that the Fed was now going to concentrate on monetary aggregates and not on interest rates. In early May 1980, Volcker eased up on the tight money growth because the actual level of the money supply, defined narrowly, declined that month. This may have been a tradeoff with President Carter, because with the monetary easing, credit controls were dropped. But by September 1980, the Fed tightened again because the money growth rate was above its target. With rising interest rates, there was more disintermediation as savers pulled their funds from financial institutions to seek higher rates in financial markets.

In addition, Volcker was concerned about more member banks

leaving the Federal Reserve System, so he strongly supported a major change in the banking laws that was passed on March 31, 1980. Many bankers and economists consider this law the most significant change in American banking since the original Federal Reserve Act of 1913. This act was called the Depository Institutions Deregulation Monetary Control Act (DIDMCA). The philosophy behind this important law was quite different from that of the 1930s changes.

Most of the banking legislation from the 1930s was designed to prevent banks from failing after about 9,000 failed in the 1929–1933 period. Congress and the public were more concerned then with insuring the safety of banks and thrift institutions than with keeping the financial system competitive and efficient. The laws enacted in the mid–1930s were still in effect almost 50 years later, when banking conditions were quite different. The twenty years following World War II, from 1945 to 1965, were generally prosperous with a relatively low rate of inflation. While the inflation rate was low, nominal interest rates were also low, so consumers and business firms were willing to hold larger cash balances than when inflation heated up in the 1970s. During the 1950s, before inflation was a problem, savings and loan associations, savings banks, and credit unions usually paid higher interest rates on savings than commercial banks, giving the alternative institutions a competitive advantage. Commercial banks, on the other hand, were the only institutions that could offer checking accounts, so they offered the public the convenience of one-stop banking, even though savings rates there were lower. Corporations often kept large amounts in non-interest checking accounts because they received favorable rates when they borrowed from the bank. Commercial banks probably felt they did not have to compete with the thrift institutions for consumer savings. The savings and loan associations, while putting almost all their assets in long-term mortgages, were able to prosper as long as they could attract enough new savings with their share (savings) accounts.

But when the rate of inflation increased from monetary expansion in the late 1960s, this secure system began to unravel. One could argue that the heavy domestic spending at the same time the nation was trying to fight a war in Vietnam caused the Fed to expand the money base excessively, but whenever the money supply grows faster than real output, prices will rise. Firms and individuals were no longer content with holding idle money balances, or with low rates on savings. Banks sought new sources of funds on which they had to pay high rates of interest. Savings banks and credit unions offered interest-bearing accounts that could compete with regular checking accounts at commercial banks. Money market mutual funds (MMMF) offered much higher rates on savings than Regulation Q allowed banks to pay, or that thrift institutions could afford to pay. They grew from $3.3 billion in deposits in 1977 to $186.9 billion in 1981. In an attempt to allow banks and thrifts to compete with these funds, the Fed and the Federal Home Loan Banks allowed banks and savings and loan associations to offer money market certificates in 1978. These certificates, which could be issued in $10,000 minimums, matured in six months and paid a rate that was tied to the Treasury bill rate. In some cases, the institutions offering these certificates found that the depositors were taking funds from lower-interest savings accounts to buy them, and thus these institutions ended up paying more for the same amount of funds. On the other hand, many depositors had less than $10,000 to invest, so they had to take their money out of these deposit institutions and invest in MMMF.

The consumer price level more than tripled from 1962 to 1982. The accompanying high nominal interest rates also caused many banks to withdraw from the Federal Reserve System. The advantages of so doing were: (1) non-member banks did not have to hold stock in the Federal Reserve; (2) some state laws allowed banks to hold lower reserve accounts than the Fed mandated; (3) some states allowed banks to hold some of their reserves in interest-earning Treasury bills. Paul Volcker, like other Fed chairmen before him, wanted to stop banks from leaving the Federal Reserve System, either because he worried over loss of monetary control, or because he wanted to protect his bureaucratic turf. A court case had challenged the right of thrift institutions to offer NOW accounts, and the court decision agreed that they were illegal. But the court gave Congress until March 31, 1980, to legalize them. The major change in banking law that did legalize NOW accounts was passed on March 31, 1980, and signed by President Carter.

This major change in banking laws was supported by Chairman Volcker and most other Fed officials. As mentioned above, it was named the Depository Institutions Deregulation, Monetary Control Act (DIDMCA). This law clearly affected commercial banks and thrift institutions more than any other legislation since the Federal Reserve Act had been passed in 1913. While important, the 1935 Amendment to the Federal Reserve Act did not affect banks as much as it did the Fed itself.

The 1980 act was trying to prevent member banks from leaving the Federal Reserve System and to make banks more competitive with non-bank competitors for savings. The provisions of this act were:

A. All banks and thrift institutions offering checkable deposits had to hold the same reserve requirements at the appropriate district Federal Reserve Bank. These requirements were 3 percent up to $56 million of deposits, and 10 percent for amounts above that.

B. All the above institutions, bank or thrift, could borrow at the Federal reserve discount window.

C. All institutions would have equal access to all Fed services such as check clearing, wire transfers, and currency delivery, but all must pay for these services. Formerly, these were offered free to member banks.

D. All institutions can offer NOW accounts and other interest-bearing checking accounts to individuals and nonprofit organizations.

E. Regulation Q and interest rate ceilings affecting thrifts are to be phased out by 1986.

F. The common reserve requirements, which were an *increase* for institutions that were *not* members of the Fed, were to be phased in by 1988. Since *the* new requirements were a *reduction* for Fed *members*, these Fed members were to be phased in by 1984.

G. Credit unions were allowed to make real estate loans, while savings and loan associations and savings banks were allowed to make consumer loans and to issue bank credit cards. Banks and thrifts were allowed to make adjustable rate mortgages, and thrifts were allowed to offer trust services. Thrifts were also allowed to hold commercial paper as an asset.

H. Deposits in banks and thrifts were insured up to $100,000 per account rather than only up to $40,000 as before.

I. The Federal Reserve board was given the power, under extraordinary circumstances, to impose an additional reserve requirement on any depository institution of up to 4 percent of its transaction accounts, but the Fed was required to pay interest on this additional reserve.

This law was supposed to give the Fed better control over the money supply by bringing all these institutions under the same reserve requirements. But it did allow a leakage by permitting all institutions to borrow from the Discount Window. This has been called a sanctioned source of slippage from a restrictive open market policy. It also was designed to make banks and thrifts more competitive with each other and with non-deposit type institutions. All savings accounts and time deposits were no longer subject to reserve requirements.

This act was passed while the Fed under Paul Volcker was trying to bring inflation down. A recession was under way in the election year of 1980, so the Fed expanded the money supply briefly after July 1980. But it did not help the incumbent president Carter, who lost to Ronald Reagan. Real output fell in 1980 while the consumer price level rose over 12 percent, so the economy was not doing well. Even after passage of DIDMCA, thrift institutions were still troubled by having to pay high interest rates to hold on to their deposits. The deep recession of 1982 caused many savings and loan associations to have a net worth that became negative.

19

Volcker's Fed Slows Inflation at a Cost

It has always been easier for an economy to experience the effects of an increase in the growth rate of the money supply than a decrease in that rate. Even if the money supply is still increasing, it can be painful to market participants if the rate of increase is dropping. Even though excessive money creation leads to inflation, the initial impact of the new money can be pleasant to those who receive it before others do. New injections of money are never distributed to everyone equally. The first recipients are usually the firms who sell their government bonds to the Fed, or those that borrow from banks that have new lending power. These firms can acquire various assets at the existing price level before the new money causes most prices to rise. On the other hand, if the Fed is slowing the growth of the money supply, firms and individuals find it harder to pay for goods. Often, borrowers have agreed in the past to pay high nominal interest rates on their debts because they anticipated even higher interest rates in the future. When the inflation rate comes down, what had been thought to be a bargain rate is no longer a good deal. The high nominal rate now becomes a high real rate, which can cause bankruptcy.

This is what the American economy faced from late 1979 through 1982. From October 1979 until March 1980, the growth of the money supply slowed, causing interest rates to go even higher as banks had to decrease their lending. This upset President Carter, who used the Credit

Control Act of 1969 to impose direct controls on various types of lending. Volcker did not like this measure, but he did not state his opposition publicly. From March to September 1980, the Fed eased up on the tightening of the money growth rate and Carter removed the credit controls. But from September 1980 through the summer of 1982, the Fed resumed its tight money policy, which caused unemployment to rise to 10 percent, making it the highest this country had seen since the 1930s. There were a many bankruptcies, especially in farming and construction. Some farmers even circled the White House with their tractors in protest. Paul Volcker, in some people's opinion, was Public Enemy Number One, and was given Secret Service protection.

Volcker believed it should take took a severe recession with high unemployment to bring down the inflation that the country had suffered for 15 years, during which the Vietnam War was waged while domestic spending was high. Volcker believed that the public must no longer expect prices to rise because when they do have those expectations, they make careless decisions in the belief that inflation will bail them out. Volcker was aware of the experience of former chairman Arthur Burns, who wanted to reduce inflation gradually but was always faced with some crisis, like the Penn Central bankruptcy or the failure of the Franklin National Bank, that caused him to ease up on the money growth rate. Volcker stood his ground until July 1982, when the Fed began to ease up, but Volcker held off the announcement that it was doing so until October 1982. That month the Fed stated publicly that it was retreating from its October 1979 policy of targeting non-borrowed reserves, and was putting less emphasis on the narrow definition of money, known as M-1.

The major Banking Act of 1980 (DIDMCA) had drastically changed what was to be counted as M-1. Formerly, this had included only currency and coin outside the banks, and checking account money on which no interest could be paid since 1933. But the 1980 act allowed many interest-earning assets to be included in the new M-1, including NOW accounts, automatic transfer services, and share drafts from both banks and thrift institutions. Because the public could now earn market rates of interest on their checkable deposits, they held more of them and fewer pure savings accounts. This increased the total of funds counted as M-1, while simultaneously causing the rate of expenditure of this new M-1 to fall below the rate that the old M-1 was spent. In other words, the velocity of M-1 was less than it had been when no interest could be paid on these funds. The Fed had to take this change into consideration when conducting its open market operations. Otherwise, keeping the new M-1 at the same growth rate of the old M-1 would cause the economy to contract severely.

While this period of tight money was being followed, Ronald Reagan became president. This brought a new philosophy of government to Washington, a philosophy very different from that of the Carter administration. The new president's advisors were all free market advocates and wanted less government control of the economy. But this did not mean that the entire administration had the same view of how monetary policy should be conducted.

Unemployment is political dynamite, and no president wants to be blamed for a Depression as Hoover was in the 1930s. During the first half of 1982, with unemployment at 10 percent, the growth rate of M-1 was 7 percent over its target rate, but real national income (GNP) had fallen 2.1 percent. The reason was that velocity had fallen, so M-1 was no longer a reliable guide to monetary policy. The Federal Open Market Committee (FOMC) had begun to use the broader definitions of money, M-2 and M-3, as monetary policy guides in the hope that they would be more closely related to nominal GNP. But by 1985, the variability of velocity had made even these measures an unreliable guide.

Volcker was now being criticized from several directions. The liberal economists, such as Nancy Teeters, had always feared the effects of a tight money policy because it hurt the housing, agriculture and small business sectors. She was often the lone dissenter under Volcker's moves to tighten money growth and increase the discount rate. Another Fed governor, Lyle Gramley, also a Carter appointee, worried about the effect of high interest rates that came with financial deregulation. Gramley believed high interest rates in the U.S. would attract foreign funds that would drive up the exchange value of the dollar, making it harder for Americans to export, and easier for foreign goods to compete with American firms domestically. He agreed with Teeters that high interest rates hurt certain sectors of the economy. He resigned from the board in 1985, a year after Teeters' term had expired.

The conservative critics of Volcker did not always agree among themselves, so they came at him from different viewpoints. The pure monetarists were usually academic economists such as Milton Friedman, Anna Schwartz, Karl Brunner, and Allan Meltzer. This group advocated a nondiscretionary monetary policy which would follow a money growth rule, because they did not believe the Fed could act in time to offset any changes it observed. In the opinion of this group, discretion almost always made the situation worse, because the Fed would act too late to have the immediate impact that was needed. But the actions the Fed took would affect the economy at a later time when the situation could call for just the opposite action.

Another group of free market economists who were affected by the severe inflation of the 1970s believed that government policy cannot influence the economy even in the short run, because the public learns to take offsetting measures to thwart the government's intentions. This group of economists believes that the public uses all available information to make rational decisions about the impact of government policy. In the late 1970s, many firms and banks employed "Fed watchers" who were experts on Federal Reserve behavior so that no monetary policy could fool their firm. For example, when the Fed expanded the money supply by open market purchases, these economists would predict a higher, not a lower, rate of interest. That is because the liquidity effect of the new money, which normally would lower interest rates, would be quickly offset by the anticipation of a higher rate of inflation, which causes nominal interest rates to rise. They further believed that any attempt to lower unemployment by monetary expansion would be quickly offset by workers demanding cost-of-living escalator clauses in their wage contracts that would prevent any price rise from lowering their real wage.

This group of economists were mainly from universities, but they had a strong influence on the Federal Reserve Bank of Minneapolis. Mark Willes, then president of the Minneapolis Fed, was the main spokesman for that bank. Willes believed that if the Fed could convince the public that it was serious about reducing the rate of inflation, it could do so without too much unemployment because workers and firms would renegotiate wage contracts to take this into effect. Some of the academic economists in this school were Robert Barro, Neil Wallace and Thomas Sargent. This "rational expectations" school also advocates a nondiscretionary monetary policy as the monetarists do.

The "rational expectations" school of economists claims that people consider all available information bearing on future consequences of their decisions. They want to avoid past mistakes. They may still make some errors but they do not keep repeating those made in the past. The public has come to believe that the government will use expansionary monetary and fiscal policy to get out of a recession, and a contractionary policy to stop inflation. But people who use rational expectations can frustrate that policy. Workers are aware that inflation from an easy money policy can reduce their real wage, so they bargain for cost-of-living escalator clauses to prevent the higher price level from reducing their real income. Unions will not enter into long term contracts in an inflationary environment that would erode their members' real income. So rational expectations can deprive the policy makers of any systematic effects. For example, an easy money policy will not lower interest rates very long because lenders will demand an inflation premium in any long-term contract. As Mark Willes has pointed out, even if individuals are not perfect forecasters, they rely on the views of experts.

The Rational Expectations School argues that there is no free ride for a policymaker even if unemployment is high, because any expansionary policy will result in higher prices. They claim that there is no critical point in the overall scale of operations that changes a quantity response to a price response. Price level changes do not occur differently when excess capacity is high or low. Spending will shift to sectors where there are fewer hindrances because the substitution possibilities are almost limitless. So these economists strongly argue against any surprise move by the Fed to change the growth of the money supply, because they believe that this will lead to greater uncertainty of prices, wages and interest rates. This will harm the economy's ability to convey information by changes in relative prices, which is the way the economy normally disseminates information.

149

A third group of free market economists also had a strong influence in the Reagan administration. These were the "supply siders," who believed that the key to prosperity without inflation is to increase the output of goods and services. Actually, this is what classical economists from the days of Adam Smith, who wrote in 1776, have always taught. The supply siders, such as Paul Craig Roberts, Arthur Laffer and Norman True, opposed Volcker's tight money policy. They wanted large tax cuts and an easy money policy because they believed that the tax cuts would unleash economic activity, which would make the economy grow out of any inflationary pressure since there would be more goods produced. In other words, the money supply would be financing a larger supply of goods, so prices would not rise the way they would if the money supply were financing the same amount of goods. Volcker got on the wrong side of these economists by suggesting that the deficit was too large and the tax cut might have been too deep.

Congress also was upset by the high unemployment in 1982 and wanted the Fed to lower interest rates. Some in Congress even threatened major changes in the Fed's structure. But once the Fed announced that monetary policy was going to be eased after mid–1982, the economy expanded with no noticeable increase in the price level. This seemed to justify the position taken by those who said that the public follows its rational expectations when considering the impact of government policy.

While most of the writings of the Rational Expectations School were originally concerned with bringing down the severe inflation of the 1970s without a large increase in the unemployment rate, the same logic applies to an economy trying to overcome a slump. These economists argued that if the public sincerely believed that the Fed were going to follow a plan to allow a slightly higher growth of the money supply, the workers would moderate their wage and price demands to keep them from being too high for the predicted money supply, and thus avoid unemployment and unsold goods. It would be in the best interest of both sides to do this. So this school of economic thought would recommend that the Fed announce a credible policy of a moderate rate of money growth and stick to it, so that unemployment could come down without a big increase in inflation.

Conversely, the rational expectationists point out that in the 1968–1969 and 1973–1974 periods, when the Fed was attempting to curb inflation, this policy surprised the public and the slower rise in the price level was accompanied with increases in unemployment. Other economists attributed the increase in unemployment to rigidity in wages that are slow to adjust downward. But the Rational Expectations School points out that higher inflation of the 1970s went with more unemployment, not less, so an announced tighter monetary policy can reduce both inflation and unemployment because it would be irrational for workers to push for higher wages at that time.

Therefore, in 1982 after three years of tight money to bring down the high inflation, it was rational for workers and firms to permit the easier monetary policy that the Fed announced to finance an increase in output without either side trying to push up wages or prices. The Fed under Paul Volcker had proven its courage to fight inflation regardless of the cost.

Another major act was passed by Congress in 1982 in reaction to the failures of savings banks and savings and loan associations. This was the Garn–St. Germain Act, which allowed banks and thrifts to offer money market deposit accounts (MMDA) to compete with money market mutual funds (MMMF). These accounts, which were covered by deposit insurance unlike MMMF, could pay whatever interest rate the bank or thrift wanted. These accounts grew to almost $400 billion by 1984, while funds in MMMF declined. In addition, thrifts were allowed to diversify their lending by investing up to 10 percent of their assets in commercial loans and up to 30 percent in consumer loans. The FDIC and FSLIC were given emergency powers to help troubled banks and thrifts to merge across state lines, so the new law encouraged interstate acquisitions of closed institutions by stronger ones. But this act also gave the impression that some banks were "too big to fail."

This 1982 act, while increasing the ability of banks to compete with mutual funds, was only a stopgap to the problem of savings and loan associations. Most of the latter were in so much trouble from being single-purpose lenders for so long that allowing them to diversify came too late for the large majority of them. They were set up to subsidize the purchase of homes, and a strong lobby of realtors, home builders, trade unions, and various suppliers all had a stake in their survival. This subsidy included the Federal Home Loan Bank System, which lent funds to meet depositor withdrawals, and the Federal National Mortgage Association, which purchased real estate loans from the savings and loans so they could make new loans. But the largest subsidy was yet to come. That came in the late 1980s when the nation's taxpayers had to pay the depositors covered by the Federal Savings and Loan Association, after the latter went bankrupt.

20

Volcker Is Reappointed but There Are Changes on the Board

With the improvement in the economy in 1983, President Reagan decided to reappoint Paul Volcker as chairman. Some of the administration's supply siders and Secretary of the Treasury Donald Regan were opposed to Volcker, but the only alternative the administration considered was Alan Greenspan. Greenspan had been former president Gerald Ford's chairman of the Council of Economic Advisors when Ford was Reagan's rival for the 1976 nomination. In addition, Greenspan did not have Volcker's international reputation at this juncture.

Volcker took the lead in working with the International Monetary Fund (IMF) and the Bank for International Settlements (BIS) in arranging for a bailout of Mexico when that country announced a moratorium on its foreign debt in 1982. It was Volcker who had to persuade Congress to increase its commitment to the IMF, and Volcker convinced Mexico of the need for a program of higher taxes and reduced spending. But Reagan's budget director, David Stockman, and his chief economic adviser, Martin Feldstein, wanted Volcker reappointed and even Alan Greenspan spoke up for Volcker, so the president asked him to stay another four years. The Senate confirmed him by an 84–16 vote. Volcker accepted even though his wife wanted him back in New York and the job was costing him financially.

But the second four years of Volcker's term would not be smooth.

President Reagan appointed four governors to the board beginning with Preston Martin in March 1982, then Martha Segar in July 1984, and finally Wayne Angell and Manuel H. Johnson in February 1986. These four were economists who wanted a more expansionary monetary policy than Volcker did, and some of them resented his autocratic style. The press referred to these supply siders as "the gang of four," a term used to describe the group that ran China's cultural revolution. In order to control the vote on the FOMC, Volcker needed the votes of the Reserve Bank presidents who agreed on a tighter monetary policy. But even though Volcker had a majority on the FOMC, he did not have a majority on the board itself. An important showdown came in February 1986 when the board voted 4 to 3 to lower the discount rate, with Volcker in the minority. Volcker was concerned that the U.S. dollar would weaken. Eventually, he was able to work out an agreement with both Germany and Japan to coordinate a reduction in their discount rates. Ultimately, Wayne Angell switched his vote to allow Volcker to work out this agreement and to prevent Volcker from resigning.

The four Reagan appointees to the board deserve to be mentioned. Preston Martin, who received his Ph.D. in economics from Indiana University in 1952, was a finance professor at the University of Southern California, and had been appointed by Reagan as the Savings and Loan Commissioner while Reagan was governor of California. Later, President Nixon made Martin chairman of the Federal Home Loan Bank Board that supervised the federally chartered savings and loan associations. His job was to deregulate the industry. He was in private industry when Reagan made him vice chairman of the Board of Governors in 1982. Initially he went along with Volcker's tight money policy, voting with the majority, but began dissenting in 1984, urging faster growth. Martin made speeches about being in a growth recession and the existence of an international debt crisis; such speeches displeased Volcker. The chairman argued that the term "growth recession" was contradictory. Volcker also objected to Martin's statement that further study of a debt-equity swap arrangement was needed to handle the international debt crisis. Volcker had already rejected the plan as unrealistic.

Preston Martin had been involved in mortgage financing before he came on the board. As a consequence of this experience, Martin recommended ways to strengthen private financing of mortgages, as a substitute for the government's involvement through the Federal National Mortgage Association and the Federal Home Loan Mortgage Association. Martin believed private firms could provide a secondary market for mortgages as the federally sponsored agencies had been doing, and that this would help stimulate home ownership. Totally private firms have since entered this field, giving credence to Martin's position. In addition, Martin was instrumental in the origination of adjustable rate mortgages, which were important in the periods when inflation was a problem.

However, when President Reagan refused to state that he would make Martin the chairman when Volcker's second term was over, Martin resigned in March 1986. He, like some other governors, was not content to be less than chairman for any length of time.

Martha Segar, who received her Ph.D. in finance and business economics from the University of Michigan in 1971, had been an economist working for the Federal Reserve board in Washington before taking positions with a commercial bank in Detroit. She was also Commissioner of Financial Institutions for the State of Michigan and held some teaching positions before President Reagan appointed her to the Board of Governors in 1984. While in graduate school, Matha Segar had been a research assistant to Paul McCracken, who was chairman of President Nixon's Council of Economic Advisors. A strong supporter of Reagan, she said she had picked up various pieces of theory from monetarists, supply siders, and even Keynesians.

She was a believer in financial deregulation and an advocate of interstate banking. Segar said she wanted further deregulation of the financial services industry. She advocated allowing banks to underwrite municipal revenue bonds and commercial paper. It was her view that banks have expertise in these fields and should not be at a competitive disadvantage with non-deposit financial institutions. She was also a very strong advocate of nationwide branch banking She was one of the four votes that wanted to lower the discount rate in defiance of Volcker, along with Preston Martin, Manuel Johnson, and Wayne Angell. Segar was quite upset when Preston Martin resigned in 1986.

Wayne Angell was named in February 1986 to fill the unexpired term of Lyle Gramley. Angell was an economist with a Ph.D. from the University of Kansas. He had been a director of the Kansas City Federal Reserve Bank and was introduced by Senator Robert Dole as a Midwesterner with an interest in agriculture. Because Angell had operated a 3,300-acre Kansas farm, Dole introduced him as a real live farmer. But in reality, Angell was mainly concerned with monetary matters as are most Federal Reserve economists. Angell took the position that the variability of the velocity of money since financial deregulation of the early 1980s had made it very difficult to control the price level by targeting some measure of money. This is because the public can now earn interest on most checking account balances, so they commingle savings and checking accounts, which makes new demand deposits a higher percentage of national income, lowering velocity.

Angell believed that the consumer price index was outdated and only available with a time lag. He suggested that the Fed look at the prices of precious metals, wheat and oil as a guide to monetary policy, because these goods were traded at auction in free markets and could thus serve as an immediate indicator of the changes in the prices of consumer goods. He felt that this commodity price index would be a better guide to short-run monetary policy because it would reflect inflationary pressures more quickly than would the consumer price index. Angell agreed with the monetarists that controlling monetary aggregates is the best way to control inflation, and this would be a better way to control money in the short run.

Manuel Johnson was an economist with a Ph.D. from Florida State University. Johnson taught at George Mason University and served in the Treasury Department under President Reagan. He stated that the monetarist's constant growth of money rule would not work with velocity as variable as it had been since the early 1980s. He said he was a supply sider in his belief that free markets are efficient, but he did not believe that all tax cuts would pay for themselves overnight by increasing the tax revenue from higher income. This view had been expressed by Arthur Laffer, a supply sider at the University of Southern California. Johnson did state that he felt a cut in the capital gains tax would lead to additional revenues to the Treasury. Another noted supply sider, Paul Craig Roberts, brought Johnson to the Treasury. Johnson advocated lower tax rates to encourage saving, and a more neutral tax structure that would not favor one type of economic activity over another. He felt that uneven tax rates lead to changes in relative prices, which cause people to make choices that they otherwise would not make. Johnson agreed with Wayne Angell that an index of freely traded commodity prices could be a short-run guide to monetary policy. He also suggested the use of the foreign exchange rate of the dollar and the relationship between short-run interest rates and long-term interest rates (the yield curve) as good guides to monetary changes because they are available on a daily basis.

During the 1980s when Manuel Johnson was under consideration by the Senate, he was asked about the impact of tax cuts on the large federal deficit, which some senators believed caused interest rates to rise. Johnson, who had been at the Treasury, responded by stating that his studies while at the Treasury could not definitely conclude that higher interest rates were caused by the deficit. Johnson carefully pointed out that other variables change. The deficit can attract foreign funds to the U.S., which can dampen the rise in interest rates. In addition, if the tax cuts effect the higher marginal rates, they could induce more saving, which could offset some of the government borrowing.

Johnson also suggested how the federal funds rate, which is the rate banks charge each other when trading in the market for excess reserves, can be a way for the Fed to control bank credit. Banks as profit-maximizing institutions will increase their lending when the rate on loans is greater than the cost of borrowed funds. They will be willing to borrow in the federal funds market when those funds can be used profitably. But if the rate on federal funds rises while the rate on loans falls, banks will more likely be willing to reduce their lending to firms and instead lend in the federal funds market. The Fed can add reserves through open market purchases of government bonds if it wishes to lower the federal funds rate, and sell bonds if it wishes to raise that rate. Even though Volcker considered Johnson a supply sider, the two worked rather well together except for a disagreement over lowering the discount rate in February 1986. But Volcker allowed a faster rate of growth of the money supply in 1986 to appease these Reagan appointees.

Bank failures became a problem during Volcker's second term as chairman. There were only 42 failures in 1982, but by 1986 this number increased to 138. Two that caught national attention were the Penn Square Bank in Oklahoma in 1982 and Continental Illinois in 1984. These two failures were connected. The Penn Square bank in Oklahoma City had made a great many loans to "wildcat" oil drillers on the assumption that oil prices would continue to rise. When oil prices fell, the bank extended its lending even though many loans were in default. Since the size of a bank's capital limits the amount it can lend to any one borrower, many of these loans were sold to Continental Illinois Bank. At that time Illinois was a unit bank state, which meant that no bank could have any branches. As the largest bank in Chicago, Continental Illinois was the recipient of a great many inter-bank deposits from smaller institutions. This bank in Chicago purchased loans from Penn Square that were not well secured, many to firms in the oil business, but also loans to underdeveloped nations.

When Penn Square failed in 1982, Continental Illinois was holding many bad loans. Over 75 percent of the deposits in this largest bank in Chicago were in accounts of over $100,000, which is the maximum that the FDIC will cover. William Isaac was the chairman of the FDIC, and as an advocate of deregulation, he believed that bank failures could serve as a lesson to reckless bankers. He did not bail out Penn Square in 1982 because he believed that corporate treasurers would discipline these wayward bankers by withdrawing their deposits gradually. But once Penn Square was allowed to fail, the large depositors panicked when they realized that Continental Illinois was in trouble. Over 2,000 smaller banks held deposits in this huge Chicago bank and they all tried to withdraw them immediately.

Unlike the bank runs of the early 1930s, which saw many small depositors lined up outside the bank trying to withdraw their savings, the bank run of the 1980s was invisible to the casual observer. Corporations and other banks with funds on deposit in the Continental Illinois could use wire transfers to move their funds elsewhere. This type of bank run also differed from those of the 1930s in that funds were not taken out in currency and kept out of the banking system, which caused the fractional reserve system to implode in the Depression. The banking system as a whole lost no funds in the 1980s when deposits were transferred to another bank. But because Continental Illinois was such a huge bank, the FDIC and the Fed considered this bank "too big to fail," which gave very large banks a competitive advantage over smaller institutions. The latter would be allowed to fail when it came to holding large corporate deposits over the $100,000 limit of FDIC insurance. The FDIC stated that they would guarantee all deposits in Continental Illinois, regardless of amount. This further proves that the FDIC is not an insurance scheme but a federal guarantee.

Between May and July 1984, over $10 billion of federal money was pumped into Continental Illinois. The FDIC assumed ownership of this institution when no bank could be found to take it over. The top managers of this failed institution were replaced but they had "golden parachutes" to avoid personal hardship. The Federal Reserve, with Volcker's approval, had to lend it about $5 billion to prevent a panic, especially among foreign investors who might assume all U.S. banks were unsafe.

Volcker did argue for nationwide branch banking after this huge failure, because it might not have happened if Continental Illinois had been able to branch around the country and diversify its lending. He also agreed with his predecessor, G. William Miller, that the Fed should pay interest to banks on their reserve accounts. But Congress was opposed to this, because it would reduce the amount of Fed earnings that would be turned over to the Treasury. Volcker was for some deregulation of banking, but not as much as the Reagan administration wanted. He did not mind banks underwriting revenue bonds issued by states and distributing mutual funds, but he opposed their underwriting corporate securities and engaging in real estate development. He also wanted to close the loophole on what were called "non-bank banks." When a court decision defined a bank as an institution that issued checkable deposits and made corporate loans, many institutions evaded banking restrictions by doing just one of those two things.

There was strong opposition in the Reagan administration to reappointing Volcker for a third term in 1987, but he had the support of both Bakers — Secretary of the Treasury James Baker and White House Chief of Staff Howard Baker. When president Reagan did offer him a third term but "without enthusiasm," Volcker resigned the next day. He may have been autocratic at times, but his strong leadership did bring down a chronic inflation that had persisted for over 15 years. He was firmly convinced that a more gradual approach would not work because some special event always comes up that requires monetary ease. The inflationary psychology had to be broken and it was broken under Volcker, even at the cost of 10 percent unemployment.

21

The Greenspan Era Begins

On August 11, 1987, President Reagan appointed Alan Greenspan to be the Chairman of the Board of Governors of the Federal Reserve System. Greenspan was a business economist who ran a consulting firm, but had taken time out from 1974 to early 1977 to serve as Chairman of the Council of Economic Advisors under President Ford. He returned to his private consulting firm when Ford left office. Greenspan was more of a free market proponent than Volcker, opposing the graduated income tax, antitrust legislation, import quotas, tariffs, guaranteed government loans to private borrowers, and consumer safety laws. He stated he was not a supply side economist, but he did have the respect and confidence of the business community.

It did not take very long for Greenspan to face a crisis. Throughout most of 1987, the Fed was concerned with controlling inflation. It was not concerned that the growth rates of the M-2 (which is a broad definition of money including many types of short-term assets) was below its target range. In September, the Fed raised the discount rate from 5.5 to 6 percent. But on October 19, the stock market dropped 508 points, losing about 18 percent of its value. The Fed immediately shifted its open market operations to providing enough reserves to satisfy the increased demand for liquidity. Short-term interest rates dropped as investors dumped stocks for safer short-term securities and to hold more transaction balances. This increased the demand for safe short-term securities, drove up their prices, and lowered their yields. The Fed made sure the supply of non-borrowed reserves was also adequate for any increase in the demand for excess reserves that banks might want to hold. After confidence was at least partially restored, the Fed resumed its goal of fighting inflation.

Another major problem that had been festering before Greenspan was appointed to the board was the savings and loan crisis. These institutions had been single-purpose lenders before the 1980s, investing all their funds in long-term mortgages because federal tax laws gave them the incentive to do that. They prospered during the 1950s in areas that were growing, such as California, because inflation and interest rates were low. They were able to attract funds by advertising all over the country, paying 4 percent on savings that were federally insured, when banks were paying less than that. They lent these savings at 6 percent for terms as long as 30 years to home buyers, and as long as new funds flowed in, they could meet depositors' demand for withdrawals.

In the 1960s, commercial banks began to compete more aggressively for savers' deposits, giving the savings and loans some competition for funds. Then in 1966, the money crunch caused by the Johnson administration trying to fight the Vietnam War, while simultaneously maintaining a high level of domestic spending, witnessed large increases in short-term interest rates. As mentioned previously, this situation occurred when Chairman William McChesney Martin refused to go along with President Johnson on an easy money policy. Depositors reacted by withdrawing funds from thrifts and banks to buy Treasury bills that were paying a higher interest rate, causing "disintermediation." While Congress passed a law in 1966 allowing savings and loans to pay ¾ of 1 percent more on savings than banks, this difference was narrowed to only ¼ of 1 percent in 1973. But the savings and loans could not offer checking accounts nor make consumer loans (on autos etc.), and were not allowed to make variable-rate mortgages at that time.

The inflation of the 1970s caused high nominal interest rates. Thus even after banks and thrifts were allowed to pay rates tied to the Treasury bill rate on six-month certificates, the savings and loan associations ended up paying more for funds than they could earn on the mortgages they held. A good part of the funds to purchase these money market certificates came from regular savings deposits, so these institutions were paying a higher rate of interest to hold on the funds they already had. Even though the new mortgages were made at high interest rates, these institutions were stuck holding many old mortgages at 6 percent that home buyers were delighted to have. But the higher deposit rates had to be paid on all deposits, or they would be moved elsewhere. This squeeze caused the market value of the savings and loan association's assets (mortgages) to fall below the value of its liabilities (deposits), which caused them to have negative net worths. Such institutions were called "zombies" because they were still operating but were legally bankrupt.

The DIDMCA of 1980 and the Garn St. Germain Act of 1982 tried to keep these thrifts operating by broadening their lending power and giving them more flexibility. But some of these institutions were too far gone for help. Nevertheless, after the passage of these two acts, thrifts could make variable-rate mortgages, offer interest-bearing checking accounts, make some consumer loans, offer trust services, buy commercial paper and low-grade "junk" bonds, and offer money market deposit accounts to compete with the money market mutual funds. In addition, the Federal Home Loan Bank Board, which then regulated the savings and loan associations, reduced their capital requirements and used a less demanding set of accounting principles as a regulatory measure. The 1982 Act allowed the Federal Savings and Loan Insurance Corporation to issue promissory notes to a savings and loan in exchange for "net worth certificates." These promissory notes from the FSLIC were listed as an asset and the net worth certificate was counted as part of the institution's capital. The weak thrifts were in fact given cash guarantees by a federal agency. The whole purpose of these "net worth certificates" was to buy time. Somehow the federal regulators were hoping for a miracle that these savings and loan associations would again be profitable.

There was a short-lived recovery for savings and loan associations from 1983 to 1985, caused in part by a law allowing faster tax depreciation for real estate, and also higher oil prices. Texas and California benefited from these two changes, as their savings and loans grew sharply in both number and in lending. But this boom quickly ended when a new tax code lengthened the tax depreciation for real estate and oil prices came down. From 1985 through 1987, over 700 savings and loan associations failed, even with the new accounting gimmicks that were allowed in the early 1980s.

A key factor in the failure of so many insured institutions was the government guarantee that goes with FSLIC insurance. This caused depositors to ignore how well an institution was run, because the government was there to pay off depositors if the thrift were to fail. This made the government insurance a moral hazard, because it gave the managers of the institution the incentive to take big risks, making them heroes if things worked out, but putting the cost of failure on the government. It also led to brokered deposits in which funds from abroad, such as those from the sale of oil, were broken down into $100,000 units and sent out to the thrifts paying the highest insured rates. The brokers involved were not concerned about how well an institution was being operated, because the government insurance was there to bail them out if it should fail.

The thrift crisis caused Congress again to pass a major act to rectify the situation. This was passed during the first year of the first Bush administration, and was called the Financial Institutions Reform, Recovery and Enforcement Act of 1989 (FIRREA). Alan Greenspan strongly advocated passage of this bill because he wanted better supervision over the thrift industry. He also wanted them to pay a higher premium for federal insurance than banks, because they had more failures and had taken bigger risks. But Greenspan firmly believed that it is right to use public money to bail out the depositors of these failed savings and loan associations, because the public has been benefiting from a stable monetary system without the fear of panicky bank runs that occurred in the 1930s, when there was a large contraction in the money supply.

The provisions of the FIRREA Act, which president George H. W. Bush signed in 1989, were as follows:

> A. The Federal Home Loan Bank Board was abolished and replaced with the Office of Thrift Supervision (OTS) under the Treasury Department.
>
> B. The FDIC was restructured into two separate funds: the Bank Insurance Fund (BIS) to insure commercial banks; and the Savings Association Insurance Fund (SAIF) for savings and loan associations.

C. The insurance premium for these two funds was almost tripled from 0.083 percent of deposits to 0.23 percent by 1991. The funds had been depleted by the large number of failures.

D. Replacing the Federal Home Loan Bank Board was the Federal Housing Finance Board to oversee the Federal Home Loan Bank System, which was retained. The new board had five members, one of which was the Secretary of Housing and Urban Development. FIR-REA had mandated that the FHLB system increase its lending to low-income people at subsidized rates.

E. This act repealed that part of the Garn St. Germain Act that allowed thrifts to invest in high-yield "junk" bonds. It also reduced the amount of funds that thrifts could invest in commercial real estate from 40 percent of assets to less than four times an institution's capital.

F. New minimum capital standards were established, and the OTS was authorized to forbid any thrift from accepting broker deposits if it failed to meet these new capital requirements.

Unlike the 1982 Garn St. Germain Act, which was a somewhat desperate attempt to keep savings and loan associations operating, the 1989 FIRREA was designed to cure the disease by closing the "zombie" institutions, and to prevent future problems in the industry that would require tax payer bailouts.

22

The Fed's Response to the Thrift Crisis

All the governors on the Federal Reserve board were vitally concerned with the problem of closing the insolvent savings and loan associations and getting the rest of them back on a sound basis, because these associations were now all able to offer checkable deposits, which had been subject to the Fed's reserve requirements since the DIDMCA of 1980. Greenspan had testified before Congress that it was essential to separate the deposit insurance for banks from that of thrifts, and to have better supervision of both types of institutions in the future. One way to implement closer supervision in Greenspan's view was to enforce higher capital requirements for these institutions, and another was to increase the deposit insurance premiums. Another Fed governor, Manuel Johnson, made the case that the existence of deposit insurance caused a moral hazard, in which the insurance allowed thrifts to take more risks that they would have if no coverage were available. He strongly advocated higher capital requirements for these troubled institutions, but also the prompt closing of insolvent ones to prevent them from living off the safety net that the insurance provides.

Most of the Fed's recommendations were adopted after FIRREA went into effect. In 1991, the Federal Deposit Insurance Corporation Improvement Act was passed, which ordered prompt action to be taken when a bank or thrift's capital falls below the prescribed level. This law also allowed the Bank Insurance Fund (BIF) and the Savings Association Insurance Fund (SAIF) to charge higher premiums to institutions that take greater risk. By the same token, it permitted lower premiums to sound institutions.

The deposit insurance fund was being rapidly depleted because of the failures of so many institutions. In 1987, the fund had a balance of $18.3 billion, or $1.10 for every $100 of insured deposits. But after four straight losing years, the fund showed a deficit of $7 billion at the end of 1991. The number of bank failures in the 1980s was very disturbing after a good record from 1945 through 1975. During that 30 year period, there were fewer than 10 failures in each of these years, and in three years (1960, 1962 and 1972,) there were none at all. But even after passage of FIRREA in 1989, there were 206 failures that year, 168 failures in 1990, 124 in 1991, 102 in 1992, but only 41 in 1993. Things improved to only 13 failures in 1994 so that the deposit insurance fund was being restored, having a balance of $21.8 billion, or $1.15 for every $100 of insured deposits. The goal set by FIRREA was $1.25 for every $100 of insured deposits so the point would soon be reached when well-capitalized, sound banks could experience a reduction in premium, while riskier institutions could expect to pay as high as 31 cents for each $100 of coverage.

As mentioned previously, when the very large Chicago bank, Continental Illinois, failed in 1984, a very unfortunate precedent was set wherein some banks were deemed "too big to fail." This gave 100 percent coverage to large corporate depositors in large banks but not for corporate deposits in small banks. It took until May 1991 for the FDIC to complete the sale of this large bank to private owners. After FIRREA was passed, the FDIC limited its payouts to covered deposits only, partly because the FDIC had just a $5 billion borrowing line from the U.S. Treasury. This borrowing line was increased to $30 billion in 1991 which permitted the FDIC to make "advanced dividend payments," beginning in March 1992, to large depositors that were over the insurance limit. This payment was usually from 50 percent to 80 percent of these claims, based on the estimated value of a failed bank's assets.

In 1994, the 13 banks that did fail did not require a direct payout from the BIF because they were taken over by other banks. In 8 of the 13 banks, depositors with accounts over $100,000 received less than the full amount, but the FDIC made "advanced dividend payments" of $8.3 million to these large depositors.

In the mid–1990s, the economy improved and banks earned better profits. In 1995, the FDIC declared that well-run banks would only have to pay 4 cents per $100 of insured deposits, which was a large drop from the 23 cents they had been paying. However, weak banks were required to continue to pay 31 cents per $100 coverage. The criteria the FDIC used to evaluate banks followed the traditional standards that bank examiners had been using for quite some time, called the CAMEL rating, which looked at Capital, Asset quality, Management, Earnings and Liquidity. The FDIC added one more to this list, S, which stood for Sensitivity to market risk.

Chairman Greenspan has been in the center of most of the publicity regarding proposed changes in the monetary system since he took over the position. His testimony before Congress and public statements have made the public aware of the problems with the banking system, and his suggestions have usually been instrumental in the legislation that brought about the recent changes. He pointed out the need to repeal that part of the McFadden Act of 1927 that limited national banks to branching only within one state, and only to the extent that state banks therein were allowed to establish branches. He successfully pointed out that this limited a bank's ability to diversify their lending industrially as well as geographically, giving American banks a competitive disadvantage.

Greenspan also opposed the "narrow bank option" as a solution to deposit insurance. This proposal wanted to have an insured bank hold only cash and government securities as assets, while the lending and investing would be done by uninsured institutions that would not be regulated. The idea was to give the public a safe asset to hold, while those with a more speculative instinct could invest in the uninsured lender with the hopes of higher returns. Greenspan argued that small banks would not compete very well against large banks under this system, and even the large banks would have trouble competing with foreign banks.

Greenspan also wanted to keep the three federal agencies (the Comptroller of the Currency, the Federal Reserve, and the FDIC) examining American banks. He liked the idea of letting a bank choose its regulator because not only would a single regulator probably end the dual banking system, which allows banks to have either a federal or a state charter, but it would also end up with more stringent controls. A bank can now change from a federal to a state charter, or vice versa, and drop out of the Federal Reserve System if it is a state-chartered bank. Over-regulation bothered Greenspan because he felt the economy needs risk taking by banks to finance more investment in new firms. He recognized the tradeoff between protecting the insurance fund and taking more risk, but he did not want to repeat the Fed's mistakes of the early 1930s when they blamed the Depression on bankers making risky loans, rather than on their own contractionary policies.

Probably most importantly, Greenspan argued successfully for the repeal of that part of the 1933 Glass Steagall Act that separated commercial banking from investment banking. This Depression-era legislation was designed to prevent banks from taking too much risk, which Congressmen at that time thought was the cause of the many bank failures. Greenspan dispelled that notion, and argued that banks can compete better and earn higher profits if they can offer more products to their customers.

Greenspan has also given his views on fiscal policy, arguing against large federal deficits, which he would like to eliminate mostly by reduced spending and not by higher taxes. He opposed a balanced budget amendment to the U.S. Constitution as being too constrictive, and also spoke out against the Treasury selling indexed bonds. Those are bonds that would rise in face value as the price level rose, as a protection against inflation. Greenspan said the Treasury should not give in to inflation, as selling these securities might indicate, and that inflation would be too hard to measure. He questioned if the Internal Revenue Service would tax this increase in nominal value, giving these securities a negative cash flow. He also considered such a security a poor device for families saving for college education because those expenses have moved up faster than the consumer price index. So far, the Treasury has followed his advice and not offered these bonds.

In September 1996, Congress passed the Deposit Insurance Funds Act, which provided for proper capitalization of SAIF by requiring the

FDIC to impose a one-time special assessment on thrift institutions to bring the SAIF up to $1.25 per $100 of insured deposits. The FDIC set this assessment at 65.7 cents per $100 covered deposits, which assessment was added to the amounts the thrifts had to pay for deposit insurance. By December 1996, the SAIF had increased its reserve ratio from 47 cents to $1.30 per $100 coverage. Thus, the FDIC lowered the annual assessment, and the deposit insurance premium was also lowered from the 23–31 cent range to 0–27 cent range. In fact, with the SAIF reserve ratio at 1.30 percent, it refunded $219 million during the last quarter of 1996.

During 1997, 1998, and 1999 bank and thrift failures were few and did not put a strain on either insurance fund. With favorable experience, about 95 percent of banks paid no deposit insurance premium in those years, and about 90 percent of the thrift institutions likewise escaped payment. This led some officials at the FDIC to be concerned. The reason was that in good times when banks could afford these premiums, none was assessed, but should bad times occur, banks and thrifts would be forced to pay more when they could least afford it. They were worried about a system that charged practically nothing in prosperous times but would have to charge a great deal in times of adversity. This concern may have been increased after the Gramm-Leach-Blily Act of 1991 repealed a part of the 1933 Glass Steagall Act that had separated commercial banking from investment banking. Investment banks help business firms sell new securities and often guarantee a certain payment to the firm, which puts the risk of selling the new securities on the investment bank. In addition to breaking down this barrier, there was some concern about the impact of international banking and the quick movement of funds across national borders. Even as the economy slowed down from its fast rate of growth in the 1990s, the banking system seemed able to withstand the recession that began in 2000.

Some of the concern that FDIC officials have about the blurring of the distinction between commercial banking and investment banking revolves around the use of deposit insurance by investment banks. These latter institutions have been able to sweep large amounts of brokerage accounts into the FDIC-insured accounts at their affiliated banks. These investment banks, however, have not paid deposit insurance premiums in the past as commercial banks have. This has allowed these investment banks to get deposit insurance coverage without the past premiums and assessments that banks and thrifts have had to make. Since both the BIF and SAIF have reached their designated legal size, the FDIC has not been collecting much in premiums because of the rebates, which are based on current assessments and not on past payments to the funds. Both the outgoing chairman of the FDIC in 2000, Donna Tanoue, and the incoming chairman in 2001, Donald E. Powell, strongly advocated allowing the FDIC to have more flexibility in managing the funds by charging premiums regardless of the size of the funds, and to issue rebates based on past payments to the fund and not on current assessments. The rebates would then go more to banks that have been stable for some time and not to fast-growing newcomers to the field.

These two chairmen also advocated allowing the deposit insurance coverage to increase with the consumer price level, since the $100,000 maximum established in 1980 is worth quite a bit less in the first decade of the twenty-first century. They also want to merge the BIF and SAIF into one fund, which they believe would be stronger than either standing by itself. The FDIC has also reported that banks, particularly the very large ones, rely much less on insured deposits as a source of funds than they did in the early 1990s. In 2001, only 50.9 percent of bank funds were derived from FDIC-covered deposits, compared to 70 percent in 1992. But for banks with assets over $1 billion, this insured amount of deposits amounted to only 46 percent of total funds, compared to 73 percent for banks under that amount.

23

Economists Dominate the Board under Greenspan

Back in the 1960s, Chairman William McChesney Martin objected to having a Board of Governors dominated by economists. But by the 1980s, it was very unusual for anyone but an economist to be nominated for governor. One member of the U.S. Senate, William Proxmire of Wisconsin, may have been one of the influential voices in changing the makeup of the board. He was the lone negative vote in the confirmation of G. William Miller as chairman in 1979, for the reason that Miller had no economic training. Miller's poor performance may also have been a strong factor in turning to economists for these important positions. Nevertheless, it is worthwhile to look at the views of the governors who have been on the board since Alan Greenspan became chairman in 1987.

Alan Greenspan was appointed by President Reagan in 1987, and reappointed by President Bush in 1992 and twice by President Clinton in 1996 and 2000. If he serves out the current four-year term that ends in 2004, he will have served seventeen years in that position, two years less than the previous record holder, William McChesney Martin, held the post. Greenspan has achieved a reputation among business leaders that would make it difficult for a president not to reappoint him even though he was born in 1926, which would make him seventy eight years old if he finishes the current term.

The few non-economists that have been on the board during the

Greenspan era have been able to function well with the other governors. Edward W. Kelley was appointed a few months before Greenspan to fill the unexpired term of economist Emmett Rice. Kelley has an M.B.A. from Harvard and ran a very successful family business in Houston before selling it and becoming the chief executive officer of Investment Advisors. As a board member, Kelley understood monetary policy well because he made use of the extensive staff of board economists. He was in favor of financial deregulation, which was an important part of the monetary changes that Congress enacted in the 1990s. He was appointed to a full term by President Bush in 1990 and served until the end of 2001.

John P. LaWare was appointed to the board by President Reagan in 1988 and served until 1995. He was a banker with an unusual academic background: a B.S. in biology from Harvard and an M.A. in political science from the University of Pennsylvania. His banking career started at Chemical Bank; and after 25 years, he became chief executive officer at Shawmut Bank. His banking experience made him believe that all financial institutions should be on an equal footing and given entrance into all areas of financial service, rather than have the absurd designation of a "non-bank bank" that evolved in the 1980s to circumvent laws passed during the early 1930s. LaWare also learned quickly the main difference between being the head man at a commercial bank and being on the Board of Governors. At Shawmut Bank he made the decisions, but at the board there was a great deal of discussion and debate about the policy to follow. But LaWare became an expert on the various types of risk that banks face: credit risk, liquidity risk, and interest rate risk. During his tenure, the amount of bank capital became an important issue during the failures of some key banks and the re-capitalization of the bank insurance funds.

The first governor appointed to the board by the first president Bush was David W. Mullins, Jr., in 1990. Mullins, with a Ph.D. in economics from M.I.T., taught at Harvard before becoming Assistant Secretary of the Treasury for Domestic Finance in 1988. He worked on the savings and loan crisis for President Bush, but his Treasury background made his confirmation hearings a little rough because some Senators felt that the Fed and Treasury should be completely separate.

174

Mullins pointed out that Governor Manuel Johnson also came to the Fed from the Treasury; Mullins also stated he definitely did not want the Secretary of the Treasury back on the board. Mullins had been Bush's point man in getting the Financial Institutions Reform, Recovery and Enforcement Act through Congress before he was appointed to the board.

As a governor, Mullins argued against a counter-cyclical monetary policy; he wanted money and credit to grow at a steady rate. At his confirmation hearings, he was asked if he were a monetarist and answered that he was a pragmatist. He recognized that the Fed had to make decisions on incomplete information, and that the effect of any policy would not be known for at least six months. He argued that the external value of the dollar should be determined by market forces and not pegged to encourage exports. A free market exchange rate would force American businesses to focus on fundamentals to be competitive. Mullins has been concerned with the short-sightedness of many decision makers resulting from the fact that American elections occur at exact intervals. He feels that the frequent changing of tax rates for political purposes can discourage saving.

Mullins has argued that the Fed should not pursue a policy of price stability but one of low or zero inflation instead. If price stability were the goal, then a supply shock that increased oil or food prices would have to be followed by a deflationary policy to knock other prices down to keep the consumer price index stable. But a policy of zero or low inflation would allow that shock to have its impact on the price index while aiming to keep the other prices relatively stable. Mullins resigned from the board in 1994.

Lawrence B. Lindsey, an economics professor at Harvard, was appointed to the board by President Bush in 1991. His confirmation took ten months because the Democratic senate felt he was too closely associated with the White House, where he had been an advisor to the president. Dr. Lindsey, who got his Ph.D. at Harvard, was the Associate Director for Domestic Economic Policy from January to September 1989, and then the Executive Director of the President's Council on Competitiveness. The Fed is not supposed to be political, while the White House is entirely political. Lindsey answered the question whether Congress should limit the Fed's independence by stating that the public should decide if that would lead to political manipulation of the money supply or not. He acknowledged that the current system of "experts" making these important decisions without being answerable to anyone can be a cause of concern.

Lindsey stated that the decade of the 1980s was a good one in that a serious inflation and deep recession were ended. He argued that the supply siders were correct about 70 percent of the time, while Keynesians were correct only about 30 percent of the time. Lindsey's main writings, including his book, *The Growth Experiment*, dealt mostly with fiscal matters, but the Fed deals only with monetary and not fiscal policy. Chairman Greenspan assigned him to head the Fed's Committee on Consumer and Community Affairs, which Lindsey did not ask for but did undertake. He had to talk banks into lending to minorities and not "redlining" certain areas of a city where they would not lend.

On purely monetary matters, Lindsey believed that the new M-2 was the best guide to monetary policy because it tracks the economy's performance better than any other indicator. He feels that tracking nominal Gross Domestic Product is a problem, because the Fed gets twelve readings a year on it (and eight are revisions of the other four.) He argues that M-2 is a good proxy for nominal GDP even if there is a distortion of 1.5 percent per year in prices, because it would allow for a real growth of income of about 3 percent if M-2 were to grow at 4.5 percent per year. He believes that monetary policy cannot influence the amount of labor and capital available, but it can improve the way those resources are used. In his view a stable, predicable economic environment helps long-run growth and encourages research and development by firms. A non-inflationary environment means investors do not have to engage in nonproductive hedging strategies to protect their wealth and can concentrate on creating wealth. Low inflation also minimizes the distortions of taxation. Dr. Lindsey resigned from the board in 1997.

Dr. Susan M. Phillips was the last of President Bush's appointments to the board in December 1991. She received her Ph.D. from Louisiana State University and was a professor of finance at the University of Iowa, specializing in commodities futures and the theory of regulation. Dr. Phillips was also on the Commodities Futures Trading Commission. She filled the unexpired term of Martha Segar. Dr. Phillips worried about the high amount of corporate and consumer debt in 1992 and advocated a tax cut stimulus to increase saving, particularly a capital gains tax cut and an investment tax credit. She agreed with most of the other governors and the Bush Administration that the Glass Steagall Act should be repealed, and that there should be less government regulation of the financial system. She argued that the "firewalls" set up by the Glass Steagall Act to keep commercial banking and investment banking separate caused inefficiencies in banking operations, which could prevent a bank from extending credit to an affiliate. Dr. Phillips left the Fed in June 1998, at the expiration of the term that began with Martha Segar.

President Clinton's first appointment to the Board of Governors came in June 1994. The person chosen was Alan Blinder, a well-known economist who was a Clinton advisor during the election campaign, and was already serving as a member of Clinton's Council of Economic Advisors. The Senate approved Blinder without the long delay that Lawrence Lindsey went through in 1991, even though Blinder had a much more political post in the Clinton Administration than Lindsey had with Bush. It may have been because the senate was controlled by the same party as the president in 1994. Blinder earned his Ph.D. at Massachusetts Institute of Technology (M.I.T.) and had been a distinguished professor of economics at Princeton University before joining the Clinton White House. Being politically in tune with Clinton, Blinder stated that he was for the underdog and wanted the government to help those who need it. But as vice chairman of the board, Blinder voted with Greenspan almost all of the time.

Blinder stated that monetarism would not be the correct philosophy to follow in the mid–1990s, but he acknowledged that it might have been in the past, and possibly in the future. He disagreed with the rational expectations school's argument that only surprises by the government can affect the economy, and he strongly rejected the Laffer Curve, wherein tax cuts would bring in more tax revenue. Blinder held that real supply side economics means that the government can do things to help the economy improve its performance by policies that encourage more production. He also believes that Keynesian economics remains viable, but agrees that its claims are much more modest than in the mid–1960s when it argued that it could fine tune the economy.

Blinder disagreed with the view that depositors should be able to have only one federally insured bank account. This idea came in the wake of the savings and loan crisis, when the insurance funds were inadequate to pay off the claims of failed institutions. It was Blinder's opinion that the public has better things to do than spending time investigating the soundness of financial institutions.

Blinder believed that the economy in 1994 had reached almost zero inflation. He felt that this would come when the public stopped worrying about it. He agreed with Governor David Mullins that attempting to stabilize the consumer price index would exact too heavy a toll, because other prices would have to be forced down if supply shocks caused some prices to rise. But in 1994 Blinder believed, as did many others, that the economy had reached its natural rate of unemployment, which was about 5.6 percent. He felt that any attempt to get unemployment lower than that by monetary or fiscal policy would cause inflation, but the unemployment rate did reach about 4.5 percent in the late 1990s without rekindling inflation. It seemed that the improvement came not from government policy, but from the workings of the micro economy, wherein the many decisions of firms and workers led to a desirable outcome.

Blinder was in a good position to contrast the workings of the Federal Reserve with that of the Council of Economic Advisors. He believed that the difference between the White House and the Fed is greater than between a university and the Fed because the White House is purely political, while the Fed engages in academic discussions similar to those at a university. According to Blinder, neither the Fed nor the university should worry about political issues, but the president and his council of advisors must be vitally concerned with them. Blinder's experience at the Fed has led him to the conclusion that the government is constantly being pushed and pulled by pressure groups to the detriment of the public. He would prefer that tax policy, like monetary policy, be transferred from Congress to a group of "experts" in a politics-free zone comparable to the Fed. He does not believe that this would weaken democracy because Congress could always take the power back. This view is the exact opposite of Milton Friedman's, who believes that it is wrong for a group of Federal Reserve governors, along with five Reserve Bank presidents who are not even politically appointed, to determine monetary policy without being subjected to elections or being replaced by political authority.

Blinder left the Fed in January 1996 when the term he was finishing expired. That was right after President Clinton reappointed Alan Greenspan as chairman. Blinder may have been disappointed that he was not offered the chairmanship.

The next governor appointed by President Clinton was Dr. Janet Yellen in August 1994. She, like Blinder, was a very well-known economist who earned her Ph.D. at Yale and was on the faculty of the University of California at Berkeley. As it turned out, she took the exact opposite road that Blinder took: She went from the Federal Reserve Board to the Council of Economic Advisors, when Clinton named her the chair of that council in early 1997. While on the board, Dr. Yellen worried about the financial markets hanging on every word uttered by a governor or some statements taken out of context. She stated that the three goals of the Fed are not paradoxical: maximum employment, stable prices, and moderate long-term interest rates. These are sensible goals that affect everyone. But the Fed is not given a guide on the tough decisions regarding choices among these goals. She agrees that there is no long-run tradeoff between inflation and unemployment, but feels the Fed can mitigate economic fluctuations by leaning against the wind, as William McChesney Martin once said. She accepts the fact that the long-run real interest rate is determined by the decisions of households, firms and the government to save and invest, and is thus outside the Fed's control. But the Fed can keep inflationary expectations down, which should keep the real and nominal rates close to each other.

Dr. Yellen stated that the severe unemployment of 1982–1983 was caused by the need to wring inflation out of the economy, and the Fed must avoid repeating that performance. So the Fed should not try to push unemployment below the NAIRU (non-accelerating inflationary rate of unemployment), or the natural rate. Such a policy creates inflationary expectations. She also acknowledges that the lags that accompany monetary policy are rather long, and that less than half the effect is felt in the first year. She credits Milton Friedman's work for warning the Fed against trying to over-steer the economy by tightening or loosening too much, and usually too late. But she disagrees with Friedman's solution of having the Fed do nothing. Rather, she feels it may be possible that when the time comes to ease monetary policy, the need will not come from current indicators but will be based on a forecast of where things are headed.

Dr. Yellen believes that Congress's only political impact on the non-political Fed comes when Congress changes banking laws. For example, she was in favor of the repeal of the Glass Steagall Act of 1933 because she felt that it would be efficient for banks to underwrite securities as long as there are appropriate safeguards. She felt that this change would benefit both industries.

As mentioned, Dr. Yellen left the Fed in early 1997 and served on the Council of Economic Advisors until the end of Clinton's term in 2001. Since that time she has co-authored a book with Alan Blinder called *The Fabulous Decade: Macro Lessons from the 1990s.* They point out that unemployment fell to a level no one thought possible and that inflation was dormant. They attribute this success to: (1) favorable supply shocks; (2) excellent monetary and fiscal policy; (3) a sharp acceleration of production after 1995; (4) reduction of the federal deficit. These two economists now believe that at least some fine tuning may be possible with skill and luck. They want the Fed to concentrate on growth more than on inflation and believe that low deficits lead to lower interest rates, which encourage investment.

The next governor appointed by President Clinton was Laurence H. Meyer, another top economist who received his Ph.D. from M.I.T. and was professor of economics at Washington University in St. Louis. He also headed his own private consulting firm in St. Louis, which specialized in macro-economic forecasting. His appointment came in June 1996; he fulfilled John P. LaWare's term which expired in 2002. During his six years on the board, Dr. Meyer served as chair of the committee on supervisory and regulatory affairs. This committee oversaw the board's implementation of the Gramm-Leach-Bliley Act, which replaced the Glass Steagall Act. Dr. Meyer also led the effort to encourage the development of sophisticated risk-management techniques at the nation's large banks. He, like many governors before him, made an effort to allow the Fed to pay interest on the reserve balances that banks hold at the Fed, as well as to get Congress to repeal the law that forbids banks to pay interest on demand deposits.

Both of the above restrictions caused wasteful efforts to circumvent them, according to Dr. Meyer. To keep reserve balances at a minimum, banks resorted to sweep accounts where funds were kept in non-reservable time deposits and then moved into demand deposits when needed. The amount of required reserves dropped from $28 billion in 1990 to $6 billion in 2000. Meyer also pointed out that required reserves are a pure monetary tool and not in any way a reserve for safety, like bank capital, which provides a buffer against losses. Meyer explained that the Fed looks to the price of reserves, which is the federal funds rate, and not the quantity of reserves. By targeting the federal funds rate, the Fed is trying to make the demand for reserves predictable. Since reserves must be maintained over a two-week period, banks have some leeway to adjust their daily balances held as reserves. If the rate on these borrowed funds is higher than usual, banks can lower their reserve balances, which decreases the demand, dampening the upward pressure on the federal funds rate.

Dr. Meyer believes that monetary policy can be a blunt instrument during a period when the economy is accelerating, as in the mid– to late 1990s. Any attempt to slow this growth can cause financial markets to put downward pressure on equities, which causes lower spending by consumers as their wealth declines. The challenge to monetary policy comes when the economy is experiencing rapid growth in productivity. Dr. Meyer does not want monetary policy to interfere with the economy in its effort to achieve a new and lower unemployment rate or a new and higher sustainable rate of output growth. During the late 1990s, he believed that this rapid increase in productivity caused a reduction in the natural rate of unemployment, at least in the short run. He feels it is unlikely that this natural rate (NAIRU) would remain steady when we move from a low to high period of growth in productivity. He now cautions that the economic slowdown in the early 2000s began with a very low rate of inflation, which was unusual. In past recessions, it was often desirable to bring down inflation as the economy slowed, but inflation was not the problem in the early 2000s. On the other hand, Dr. Meyer warns that we must be careful in applying anti-recession tools, so that we do not create conditions for future inflation. In his opinion, monetary policy is a potent tool to maintain a low rate of inflation.

Dr. Alice Rivlin was appointed to the Federal Reserve board by President Clinton one day after Laurence Meyer, on June 25, 1996. Dr. Rivlin got her Ph.D. in economics from Harvard University and taught at George Mason University before becoming Director of the Congressional Budget Office from 1975 through 1983. She advocated deficit reduction. After that, she worked with the Office of Management and Budget in the Clinton administration. With that background, she was assigned as the governor responsible for the Federal Reserve board's budget. She also worked with Governor Laurence Meyer on implementation of the Community Reinvestment Act. In 1992, Dr. Rivlin wrote *Reviving the American Dream* in which she argued that too many working families are not experiencing an increase in their real incomes. She also feels that state and local governments make a mistake in trying to compete for new jobs by offering lower taxes. She would prefer to see states work together on a regional basis toward improving their services and infrastructure.

On November 5, 1997, President Clinton made his last two appointments to the Board of Governors, and again they were economists with excellent reputations. They were Dr. Edward M. Gramlich and Dr. Roger W. Ferguson, Jr. Dr. Gramlich, who got his Ph.D. in economics from Yale, was professor of economics and later dean at the University of Michigan. He replaced Janet Yellen, so his term ends in 2008. He is a strong advocate of free trade and the free flow of capital internationally where it can get the highest return. He has also made clear his choice for reforming social security: 1) reduce some benefits to the wealthy but not to the poor; 2) make all new state and local government workers join the system; 3) increase the retirement age slightly; 4) have high-wage workers contribute 1.6 percent of their pay to a new individual account that would be invested in the mutual fund of that person's choice.

Dr. Roger Ferguson has earned all his degrees from the University of Michigan, including a law degree as well as his Ph.D. in economics. He has already been reappointed by President George W. Bush for a full fourteen-year term that will expire in 2014. He is now the vice chairman and has been concerned mainly with international financial stability. He has chaired the Financial Stability Forum. He made it plain in a speech before M.B.A. graduates at Washington University in St. Louis that the most important thing the Fed can do is to keep inflationary expectations under control. He stated that the Fed's control over the size of its balance sheet determines the value of the nation's money and the long-run price level. This helps private decision makers (households and firms), act as efficiently as possible because they can save, invest and produce without concern over changes in the price level. Long-term interest rates will not contain inflation premiums. But he pointed out that the Fed cannot totally eliminate risks that are part of private decision making. He also noted that prices in 2003 are increasing at the lowest rate in over 30 years, but he believes that the possibility of deflation is very remote.

As mentioned above, the six governors appointed by President Clinton all had Ph.D.'s in economics and were extremely capable. Alan Blinder, Janet Yellen and Alice Rivlin would probably vote differently than Alan Greenspan and some of the Bush and Reagan appointees if they were in Congress, but none of the governors appointed by Clinton voted against Greenspan at FOMC meetings. It seems that economists, regardless of their political views, have come to realize the importance of preventing a serious inflation that the country experienced in the 1970s. There also seems to be a consensus that monetary policy can only affect nominal values in the long run (ie. the price level), so the best way to help the economy to grow and prosper is to keep money from being a source of disturbance.

Besides reappointing Dr. Roger Ferguson as governor, President George W. Bush has appointed three other people to the Board of Governors since he has been in office. Dr. Susan S. Bies has a Ph.D. in economics from Northwestern University and was vice president of First Tennessee Bank in Memphis, specializing in risk management. Her term expires in 2012. Dr. Ben S. Bernanke was appointed to a fulfill a term expiring in 2004. Dr. Bernanke has a Ph.D. in economics from M.I.T. and was a professor at Princeton University. Dr. Donald L. Kohn was appointed to a full term ending in 2016. Dr. Kohn earned his Ph.D. in economics from the University of Michigan and has spent most of his professional life working for the Federal Reserve. He was with the Kansas City Federal Reserve Bank from 1970 through 1975 and has been a research economist with the Board of Governors from 1975 through 2002. Mr. Mark W. Olson was appointed to a term that expires in 2010. Mr. Olson has a bachelors degree in economics from St. Olaf College in Minnesota, and was president and chief executive office of Security State Bank in Fergus Falls, Minnesota from 1976 through 1988. For the next eleven years, he was a partner with Ernst and Young before becoming staff director of the securities subcommittee of the Banking, Housing and Urban Affairs Committee of the U.S. Senate. This subcommittee was concerned with the Securities and Exchange Commission and held oversight hearings on the Gramm Leach Blily Act. Even though Mr. Olson is the only board member who does not have a Ph.D. in economics, he has extensive experience in banking, which should be an asset in his position.

24

Changes in the Fed's Operating Procedure after the 1980s

The Fed was able to bring down the severe inflation of the 1970s by a tight money policy under the regime of Paul Volcker in the 1980s. But after the passage of the DIDMCA of 1980, the definition of what had been classified as money changed. Even after significant tax cuts were enacted in the early 1980s, inflation did not reoccur when the money supply, defined as M-1, was allowed to grow sharply after mid–1982. Some prominent monetarists, such as Milton Friedman, predicted that inflation would become a problem with such an easy money policy, but the inflation rate came down from 1982 through 1987 even with the fast growth in money. One probable cause of this change in the relationship between the supply of money and total income (Gross Domestic Product) has been the inclusion of savings balances in M-1, which formerly contained only transaction balances. With this change, the public is holding more money in the newly defined M-1 than they held in the old M-1, which contained only currency, coin and demand deposits, that paid no interest. Therefore, the demand for the new M-1 is much greater than it was for the old M-1, which makes the ratio of M/GDP larger than before.

Putting it another way, the velocity of money has fallen. From 1960 through 1980, velocity rose as interest rates rose along with the rate of inflation. Money was not a good asset to hold, so the public tried to keep its M-1 balances at a minimum. But after 1980, not only did the inflation rate come down, but the public, other than corporations, could earn a market rate of interest on its money holdings. This decrease in velocity meant that the Fed could no longer rely on a money growth rule to conduct monetary policy. After 1987, the Fed stopped setting M-1 targets but also found M-2 and M-3 unreliable. Most of the funds in M-2 and M-3 are not subject to reserve requirements. It appeared that the Fed was relying on short-term interest rates, particularly the federal funds rate.

Alan Greenspan testified in July 1993 that the historical relationships between money and income and money and the price level have broken down, depriving these aggregates of much of their usefulness as guides to policy. The aggregate M-2 was downgraded and there did not appear to be any single variable to take its place. While he said that the FOMC never adhered to a narrow path for M-2, the persistent deviations of this variable from its expected value were a warning that monetary policy may not be achieving its desired results.

Another factor that could change the ability of banks and thrifts to keep lending if interest rates should rise has been the abolishment of Regulation Q, which formerly limited what these institutions could pay on their deposits. In the future, if interest rates were high and rising, banks could keep from losing funds by paying whatever it took to retain them. But since inflation has come down the past 20 years, there is no longer an inflation premium built into interest rates, so this situation has not occurred.

When inflation was rampant in the 1970s, a school of economists argued that inflation could be brought down without significant increases in the unemployment rate if the Fed could convince the public that it was absolutely determined to stop the rise in the price level. This school of thought believed that an informed public would form rational expectations about the future levels of inflation and unemployment. After Paul Volcker's regime brought down the chronic rate of inflation by a tight money policy from 1979 to mid–1982, it seemed that the Fed would not back off this restrictive policy even in the face of 10 percent unemployment. Once the pubic realized that the Fed was sincere in its anti-inflation effort, it no longer expected an easy money policy. Rationally, workers lowered their wage demands and large firms moderated their pricing policies. Even with the higher rate of money growth, because of the new definition of M-1, the lower expectation of inflation allowed unemployment to come down without a rekindling of inflation.

The procedure that many economists, including some who are employed in research positions with the Federal Reserve, believe has guided Fed policy is the "John Taylor Rule." Taylor, a Stanford professor, has developed a rule encompassing the rational expectations belief in the lack of any tradeoff between inflation and unemployment. This rule, simply stated, calls for the real federal funds rate to be increased 0.5 percentage point if real income rises 1 percentage point above potential income (GDP), and should also be increased 0.5 percentage point if the inflation rate rises 1 percentage point above its target of 2 percent per year. But the real federal funds rate should be lowered if inflation is below the 2 percent target rate, or if unemployment is above the natural rate (NAIRU). According to Taylor, when actual GDP is equal to potential GDP, and inflation is 2 percent per year, the federal funds rate should be about 4 percent, which would be a 2 percent rate in real terms.

Taylor's research reveals that monetary policy should be conducted according to a rule that everyone understands. This would give credibility to Fed policy and allow the public to form its future plans rationally without worrying over the probability of future inflation. Taylor also believes that such a rule would improve the Fed's policy performance by making the Fed more accountable, and would help new members of the Open Market Committee learn the job quicker. However, Taylor does leave some room for Fed discretion. He acknowledges that some special event could require departure from the rule. Examples would be the stock market meltdown on October 19, 1987, or the national calamity that occurred on September 11, 2001. But with a rule in place, any discussion about deviating from the rule would be more likely to focus on the rule than on pure discretion.

Taylor's rule clearly provides recommendations for the Fed to set the short-term federal funds rate as conditions change, so that it can hit its short-run goal of economic stabilization and also its long-run goal of controlling inflation. Taylor makes it clear that increases in the real federal funds rate must be greater than the natural rate of interest when inflation heats up, if we are to avoid the inflation spiral of the 1970s. This is because the nominal interest rate normally rises one for one with anticipated inflation, so if the federal funds rate were only raised one for one, it would not have a restraining impact on the economy. To stop the inflation, the Fed must raise the real, not just the nominal, federal funds rate. Currently, the low federal funds rate would be consistent with an economy below its full employment level. The response of the Fed to an output gap should stabilize the economy according to the rational expectations school, and not lead to misguided self-fulfilling expectations of inflation, as happened in the 1970s. As mentioned previously, when the Fed under Paul Volcker announced an easier monetary policy in late 1982 after almost three years of tight money, unemployment fell and output increased without any significant increase in the rate of inflation.

Federal Reserve Governor Edward M. Gramlich in a 1999 speech at the Wharton School in Philadelphia stated that the sharp change in velocity that has occurred after passage of the DIDMCA of 1980 has changed the Fed from a quantity-of-money watcher to an interest rate watcher. This is consistent with traditional monetary theory, which states that if the demand for money is more unstable than fluctuations in real output, targeting an interest rate is preferable to targeting the money supply. Just the opposite is true if real output fluctuates more than the demand for money. In referring to the Taylor rule, Gramlich said that estimating the equilibrium real federal funds rate or the natural rate of unemployment are not easy because changes in productivity or in the national savings rate could affect each. He pointed out that the actual unemployment rate in the late 1990s fell below what economists had previously believed would be the natural rate, yet inflation did not accelerate. So the Fed would not have wanted to raise the federal funds rate to increase unemployment to what had been thought was the natural rate.

Governor Gramlich takes the position that if the unemployment rate were dropped from the Taylor rule, it would become close to a inflation-targeting rule. He suggests converting it to a change rule wherein monetary policy can try to keep inflation and unemployment within the target bounds. Policy could then respond only when movements in the economy took inflation or unemployment out of these bounds. He suggested trying to grow aggregate demand equal to the growth rate of aggregate supply, which is more predictable. Since aggregate demand has now fallen below the growth of aggregate supply, monetary policy should boost the growth of demand by lowering the federal funds rate.

In a speech before the Allied Social Science Association in Washington, D.C. in January 2003, Gramlich stated that the long-run goal of the Fed is to avoid inflation or deflation. He did acknowledge that the Fed has a goal of maximum sustainable employment. Gramlich stated the Fed should respond to short run fluctuations in unemployment by lowering the federal funds rate. In addition to the John Taylor Rule, Gramlich stated that the Fed is following an operation called "Flexible Inflation Target," or FIT. This policy announces an inflation target and tries to hit it over a two-year period, but the targeting is flexible to allow for response to supply shocks. Because monetary policy operates with a lag of about 18 months, FIT allows the Fed to be ahead of the curve. He reiterated the theory that if real spending shocks occur, the Fed should target money, but if money demand shocks occur, the Fed should target interest rates. The demand for money, however, is much harder to observe. He also stated that the Fed should not operate in secret. He was pleased that the Fed has been making the results of FOMC meetings public immediately since early 1994.

Two research economists at the San Francisco Federal Reserve Bank, John Judd and Glen Rudebusch, tried to estimate how the Fed, under three different chairmen, altered monetary policy in response to changes in the economy. Using the rational expectations model and applying Taylor's rule, they found that Alan Greenspan's policy was consistent with a low inflation rate and a stable output. But they found that the federal funds rate under Greenspan reacted twice as strongly to gaps in output as the Taylor rule would assume. But the changes in that rate have moved gradually and not abruptly. Under Volcker, the federal funds rate was changed gradually to achieve an inflation rate well below the one he inherited when he took over in the fall of 1979. This was consistent with his goal of reducing inflation. But under

Arthur Burns, there was a weak response to inflation. His policy seemed to be concerned with the phases of the business cycle, which was consistent with the high rate of inflation that was experienced in the 1970s.

Two economists, Laurence Ball and Robert R. Tchaidze, applied the Taylor rule to the 1990s and found that the rule breaks down if it is based solely on the inflation rate and the unemployment rate. But they found that the Fed's behavior appears to be stable if we account for the falling natural rate of unemployment (NAIRU). A rule based on inflation and the deviation of unemployment from the NAIRU explains the Fed behavior during the Greenspan era between 1987 and 2000. They attribute the more sophisticated monetary policy to the use of the Fed's "Green Book," which is compiled by the large staff of economists who work at the Board of Governors. Using the Green Book allows the Fed to take into account expected future developments regarding real spending and price shocks, and allows the board to obtain better forecasts of future output.

Professor John Barro of Harvard University was one of the main researchers in the 1970s that expounded the "rational expectations" theory. He criticizes that part of the Taylor rule that calls for higher interest rates when the level of income rises above the natural rate. Barro's studies do not predict more inflation when the real income grows, so he would prefer that the Taylor rule be just an inflation-controlling rule. So Professor Barro would raise the short-term rate when inflation heats up but not when real income grows. Barro attributes the growth in real income in the late 1990s to strong technological progress, expansion of global markets, and reductions in world wide inflations.

Two research economists at the Cleveland Federal Reserve Bank, Charles Carlstrom and Timothy Fuerst, look upon the Taylor rule as simply an important *guidepost* for monetary policy because the Fed officials do not like to be restrained by a *rule*. Since the Taylor rule was proposed in 1993 and based on pre–1993 data, they have tried to see if it has defined Fed policy in the last ten years since 1993. Their findings are that it has not been as reliable a guide since then. But they believe that even though other things can affect monetary policy, the Fed should respond only to changes in inflation and output. They showed that the federal funds rate was above what the Taylor rule would have predicted in the late 1990s, even though output increased. Carlstrom and Fuerst state that this period saw an increase in productivity that leads to faster growth in real income, which in turn leads to higher real interest rates. The Fed apparently felt the higher productivity was permanent, so they adjusted the Taylor rule upward.

Carlstrom and Fuerst in 2003 explain why monetary policy appears to be easy with the federal funds rate so low. They explain this by the large decrease in equity prices that seems unprecedented, and the disaster that occurred on September 11, 2001, with the necessary step-up in security measures. So the Taylor principle can be adjusted for inflation targets other than 2 percent annually. They reiterate that if the Fed's potential guideposts can be explained by the Taylor principle, this will give the Fed important credibility that would allow them to deviate from a strict rule in the short run in response to unforeseen events without risking inflation.

In 2003, some people were concerned that the Fed might have to deal with a problem it has not encountered in over 70 years: deflation. Some observers looked at the federal funds rate, which was nearing 1 percent, and asked if it could go much lower if the producer price index were to fall. Alan Greenspan answered by saying that the Fed could buy long-term government bonds which would drive up their price and lower their yield. This would be an occasion on which the Fed could use some discretion. It would also show that the Fed would never again be tied to a "bills only" policy as they had limited themselves to in the 1950s.

Some other Fed governors have weighed in on the possibility of deflation, and the current recession that began in 2000. Edward Gramlich stated that if deflation did occur, and short-term interest rates were near zero, the Fed would then target the money supply to ensure a more expansionary policy. A rapid increase in liquidity would arrest the deflation. Vice Chairman Roger Ferguson, Jr., stated that the three objectives of Fed policy (maximum employment, stable prices, and moderate interest rates), have collapsed into a single goal as the dismal experience of the 1970s taught us. Stable prices cause firms and households to focus on producing, saving and investing without concern for inflation, which removes the inflation premium from interest rates.

Professor Barro therefore would prefer that the Taylor rule be just an inflation-targeting rule as Governor Gramlich referred to his speech. On the other hand, Barro does not believe there is a danger of deflation, even though he advocates an increase in aggregate demand.

The increased labor productivity we are now experiencing helps employed workers, but it can make it harder for the unemployed to find jobs. Both governors Mark V. Olson and Susan Bies have stated that this recession is one of the few that started by a decrease in business investment, rather than by households cutting their spending. Current excess capacity can hurt investment recovery although the low interest rates have helped the housing sector and consumer durables. But the inability of firms to raise prices has caused them to concentrate on being more efficient and cutting costs including labor costs, which can prolong unemployment. But all Fed officials have stated that the banking system is healthy and can deal with any problem of deflation.

It should be clear that there is no connection between the current situation and the early 1930s. That period was one of banking collapse when bank runs were contagious and the Fed allowed the money supply to fall by one-third over the 1929–1933 period. Any mild drop in prices now is a reflection of increased productivity at a faster rate than the growth of total demand. But the money supply is not falling and the banks are generally sound.

Conclusion

The recent record of the Federal Reserve has been much better than its very poor performance in the 1930s when it allowed the money supply to fall by one-third, and in the 1970s when it permitted a near doubling of the money supply. One very significant change over the years has been the type of people who have been placed on the Board of Governors and also in the position of district Reserve Bank presidents. Almost all the governors now are either professional economists or at least very well trained in economics. This is quite a contrast from when the original members of the Federal Reserve board were supposed to represent various sectors such as agriculture, industry and banking.

This brings us to a major difference in political and economic philosophy between two top and very able economists, Milton Friedman and Alan Blinder. Milton Friedman believes that the government is too powerful and intrusive into the lives of its citizens. He wants the role of government limited in order to increase the free choices the public can make on its own behalf. Alan Blinder believes that government is not too big but rather, is being pushed and pulled by various pressure groups who want to further their own ends. This major difference in philosophy causes them to offer almost opposite suggestions of how monetary policy should be conducted.

Milton Friedman has stated that, while at the University of Chicago, the hardest thing for him to explain to intellectuals in other departments was that twelve people sitting around a table in Washington can determine our money supply and not be subject to election, dismissal, nor close political or administrative control. He believes that this power is too important to be exercised by these few people because of the huge mistakes made in the early 1930s that plunged the nation into a deep depression and the severe inflation their actions caused in the 1970s.

Alan Blinder, on the other hand, was on the Board of Governors in the 1990s when monetary policy performed as well as it ever had. He therefore likes the independence the Fed has, and would like this independence extended to the makers of fiscal policy, which is now exercised by Congress through its taxation, borrowing and spending. Blinder trusts intellectuals to do what is "right and good" for the nation, while Friedman feels that well-intended people can often do more harm that those who set out purposely to do evil. So while Blinder would allow Fed officials to have complete discretion, Friedman would want them constrained by a money growth rule that Congress would mandate.

One view of monetary policy that was heard in the 1930s and 1940s was that monetary policy is much stronger in combating inflation than in overcoming depressions or recessions. The thought was that a reduction in the money supply or in its rate of growth would cause people to rein in their spending. In a downturn the Fed can put new reserves into the banking system via open market purchases of government securities, but these reserves may go unused if the public does not want to borrow from the banks. The analogy used by the then-chairman of the Board of Governors, Marriner Stoddard Eccles, was that "monetary policy is like a string: you can pull on it but you can't push on it." That analogy was dispelled by the evidence of monetary researchers (such as Milton Friedman, Anna Schwartz, and Clark Warburton), that showed that, contrary to popular thinking, monetary policy was very tight in the 1930s, not easy as some Keynesian economists taught. The confusion stemmed from the fact that short-term interest rates were very low in the 1930s because banks and firms were holding Treasury bills as a safe asset. This drove up the price of those bills, and lowered their yield to almost zero. But long-term bonds, which were considered risky, were often shunned by investors, and hence had higher yields and lower prices. Keynesian economists mistook the low yield on Treasury bills for an easy monetary policy, seeming to ignore the supply of money.

At the present time in 2003, the Fed has been trying to combat a recession by following a low-interest rate policy, using the federal funds rate as a target. It now seems that there is strong agreement that the Fed can keep inflation in check by controlling the amount of money circulating in the economy. However, the other goal of the Fed, maximum employment, is not something that can be achieved by targeting the federal funds rate. This depends instead on the decisions of business firms, investors, savers, and workers. The Fed knows that the best environment to enable the private sector to provide growth in jobs and output is a money supply that is adequate for financing this growth, but not excessive so as to cause a rekindling of inflation. Fiscal measures such as unemployment insurance can help alleviate the stress of job loss. This help was not available to the unemployed in the early 1930s.

Some of the mystery has been taken out of monetary policy during the past few years. Since 1994, the FOMC has made public its policy recommendations immediately, rather than keeping them secret for a lengthy time. The reason for the secrecy was to prevent investors from gaining inside information, but this was found to be less of a problem than the guesswork of professional "Fed-watchers," hired by banks and private firms. The other measure taken recently has been tying the discount rate to the federal funds rate, making it one percentage point higher. In this way, there is no longer an announcement effect when the rate is changed, and it becomes a penalty rate rather than a subsidy to banks. The Fed would then be a true lender of last resort not a lender of first resort as it was when the discount rate was below the federal funds rate.

The success the Fed has had in the 1990s in stemming inflation has reduced the clamor to abolish or greatly alter the Fed. When inflation was chronic in the 1970s, many economists expounded the virtues of alternative monetary regimes. One plan by Murray Rothbard was a 100 percent gold dollar, where all money (currency or deposits), could be exchanged one for one with gold. Rothbard believed that central banks inflate the money supply, lowering the wealth of money holders. He also believed that banks should hold 100 percent gold reserves for all deposits, making the depositor a bailor and the bank a bailee similar to the relationship of a farmer and a grain elevator. In his plan, there would be no central bank and no institution to conduct monetary policy.

Milton Friedman also wanted banks to hold 100 percent reserves for deposits, but his plan did not call for gold reserves. Banks would hold reserves either in vault cash or on deposit at the Federal Reserve equal to demand and time deposits. The Fed would pay market rates of interest to the banks on these reserves, so that the banks could pass most of this interest on to depositors. This would make it less likely that banks would try to evade the requirement. The Fed would then be like a computer, having no discretionary power, restricted to increasing the money supply, day by day at an annual rate of 3 or 4 percent, which would allow prices to be reasonably stable. Banks in both Rothbard's plan and Friedman's plan would obtain loanable funds by offering the public various forms of debt or equity that would transfer the purchasing power from the depositor to the bank. Then when the bank made a loan, the purchasing power would move from the bank to the borrower, and no money would be created in the lending process.

Several other economists (Lawrence H. White, George Selgin, Charles Goodhart, Kevin Dowd, and David Glasner) suggested a plan of free banking with no government regulation. Their main thesis is that if the free market can give us food, clothing and shelter, it can give us a money that would not lose value. Free banking would put no restrictions on entry into the banking industry nor any limitations on non-fraudulent banking practices. Each bank would be free to hold any type of asset, to acquire funds through any type of liability, and to establish branches wherever it chose. Banks would not be subject either to legal reserve requirements or to minimum amounts of capital, and would issue their own distinctive bank notes which would serve as currency if the public would accept them. It is very likely that banks would be forced by competition to convert their notes and deposits into some reserve asset, such as gold or silver or the frozen supply of Federal Reserve Notes, on demand. The frozen federal reserve notes would serve a role similar to what the frozen supply of greenbacks did after the Civil War. Banknotes, like deposits, would be "inside" or bank-issued money, not "outside" or reserve money as federal reserve notes are now.

No free bank would have a monopoly of the note issue as central banks have, and no bank would have the protection of legal tender laws, forcing acceptance. Free banks can only put their money into circulation if the public wants to hold it. Any unwanted bank notes and deposits return quickly to the issuer. Hence, unlike a central bank, no free bank can influence the price level. Free banks, unlike commercial banks today, can handle any demand for currency by exchanging one liability for another, deposits for bank notes, without disturbing their assets. In addition, unissued bank notes make an inexpensive vault cash because they are not a liability until issued.

Competing monies in the form of bank notes do have relative prices that can make one more desirable than the other. But when a central bank has a monopoly of the note issue, and all bank deposits are exchangeable into this Federal Reserve Note, then serious consequences will occur if the supply of this money and the demand for it are not equal. The reason is that with a monopoly money, it has no price of its own as do all other goods in our economy. Therefore, if the demand for any other good, even an asset very close to money such as a Treasury bill or, at the opposite extreme, an original painting, were greater than the supply, that good's price would rise to clear the market. But if the demand for a monopoly money issued by a central bank were greater than its supply, the public would contract their spending, attempting to hoard money. Then the only way the market could clear with no increase in the supply of this money would be for prices and incomes to fall low enough to reduce the demand. Money is one good that the public can demand merely by not spending it.

This point was made by Professor Leland Yeager, who also shows what happens when the supply of money is greater than the demand for it. In that case, the public spends its unwanted balances but in the aggregate they do not go away. Money moves from one person to another, driving up incomes and prices until it is wanted to support the higher level of incomes and prices. So the conclusion to be drawn from this is that a central bank can increase its money and people will accept it even if they do not want to hold it. The supply of Fed money will eventually create its own demand.

Hence, we must be aware that even if the Fed has performed very well recently, we are at its mercy if it wants to inflate or deflate. It is unlikely that the Fed would want to do bad things on purpose, but it did them accidentally in the 1930s and again in the 1970s, and we all had to suffer.

Appendix A: Membership of the Board of Governors of the Federal Reserve System, 1913–2003

Name	Federal Reserve District	Appointed By President	Term Served
Charles S. Hamlin	Boston	Wilson	1914–36
Paul M. Warburg	New York	Wilson	1914–18
Frederic A. Delano	Chicago	Wilson	1914–18
W. P. G. Harding	Atlanta	Wilson	1914–22
Adolph C. Miller	San Francisco	Wilson	1914–36
Albert Strauss	New York	Wilson	1918–20
Henry Moehlenpah	Chicago	Wilson	1919–20
Edmund Platt	New York	Wilson	1920–30
David C. Wills	Cleveland	Wilson	1920–21
John R. Mitchell	Minneapolis	Harding	1921–23
Milo D. Campbell	Chicago	Harding	1923–23
Daniel R. Crissinger	Cleveland	Harding	1923–27
George R. James	St. Louis	Harding	1923–36
Edward Cunningham	Chicago	Harding	1923–30
Roy A. Young	Minneapolis	Coolidge	1927–30
Eugene Meyer	New York	Hoover	1930–33
Wayland W. Magee	Kansas City	Hoover	1931–33
Eugene R. Black	Atlanta	Roosevelt	1933–34
M. S. Szymczak	Chicago	Roosevelt	1933–61
John J. Thomas	Kansas City	Roosevelt	1933–36
Marriner S. Eccles	San Francisco	Roosevelt	1934–51

Name	Federal Reserve District	Appointed By President	Term Served
Joseph Broderick	New York	Roosevelt	1936–37
John K. McKee	Cleveland	Roosevelt	1936–46
Ronald Ransom	Atlanta	Roosevelt	1936–47
Ralph W. Morrison	Dallas	Roosevelt	1936–36
Chester C. Davis	Richmond	Roosevelt	1936–41
Ernest G. Draper	New York	Roosevelt	1938–50
Rudolph Evans	Richmond	Roosevelt	1942–54
James Vardaman	St. Louis	Truman	1946–58
Lawrence Clayton	Boston	Truman	1947–49
Thomas B. McCabe	Philadelphia	Truman	1948–51
Edward L. Norton	Atlanta	Truman	1950–52
Oliver S. Powell	Minneapolis	Truman	1950–52
William McC. Martin	New York	Truman	1951–70
A. L. Mills, Jr.	San Francisco	Truman	1952–65
J. L. Robertson	Kansas City	Truman	1952–73
Candy Balderston	Philadelphia	Eisenhower	1954–66
Paul E. Miller	Minneapolis	Eisenhower	1954–54
Charles Shepardson	Dallas	Eisenhower	1955–67
G. H. King, Jr.	Atlanta	Eisenhower	1959–63
George W. Mitchell	Chicago	Kennedy	1961–76
J. Dewey Daane	Richmond	Kennedy	1963–74
Sherman Maisel	San Francisco	Johnson	1965–72
Andrew Brimmer	Philadelphia	Johnson	1966–74
William W. Sherrill	Dallas	Johnson	1967–71
Arthur F. Burns	New York	Nixon	1970–78
John E. Sheehan	St. Louis	Nixon	1972–75
Jeffrey Bucher	San Francisco	Nixon	1972–76
Robert C. Holland	Kansas City	Nixon	1973–76
Henry C. Wallich	Boston	Nixon	1974–86
Phillip E. Coldwell	Dallas	Ford	1974–80
Phillip Jackson Jr.	Atlanta	Ford	1975–78
J. Charles Partee	Richmond	Ford	1976–86
Stephen Gardner	Philadelphia	Ford	1976–78
David M. Lilly	Minneapolis	Ford	1976–78
G. William Miller	San Francisco	Carter	1978–79
Nancy H. Teeters	Chicago	Carter	1978–84
Emmett J. Rice	New York	Carter	1979–86
Frederick Schultz	Atlanta	Carter	1979–82
Paul A. Volcker	Philadelphia	Carter	1979–87
Lyle Gramley	Kansas City	Carter	1980–85
Preston Martin	San Francisco	Reagan	1982–86

Name	Federal Reserve District	Appointed By President	Term Served
Martha R. Segar	Chicago	Reagan	1984–91
Wayne D. Angell	Kansas City	Reagan	1986–94
Manuel H. Johnson	Richmond	Reagan	1986–90
H. Robert Heller	San Francisco	Reagan	1986–89
Edward Kelley Jr.	Dallas	Reagan	1987–01
Alan Greenspan	New York	Reagan	1987–
John P. LaWare	Boston	Reagan	1988–95
David Mullins, Jr.	St. Louis	Bush	1990–94
Lawrence Lindsey	Richmond	Bush	1991–97
Susan M. Phillips	Chicago	Bush	1991–98
Alan S. Blinder	Philadelphia	Clinton	1994–96
Janet L. Yellen	San Francisco	Clinton	1994–97
Laurence Meyer	St. Louis	Clinton	1996–02
Alice M. Rivlin	Philadelphia	Clinton	1996–99
Roger Ferguson Jr.	Boston	Clinton	1997–
Edward M. Gramlich	Richmond	Clinton	1997–
Susan S. Bies	Chicago	Bush	2001–
Mark W. Olson	Minneapolis	Bush	2001–
Ben S. Bernanke	Atlanta	Bush	2002–
Donald L. Kohn	Kansas City	Bush	2002–

Appendix B: Persons Serving as Chairman of the Board of Governors

Name	Term of Chairmanship
Charles S. Hamlin	Aug.10, 1914–Aug. 9, 1916
William P. G. Harding	Aug. 10, 1916–Aug. 9, 1922
Daniel R. Crissinger	May 1,1923–Sept. 15, 1927
Roy A. Young	Oct. 4, 1927–Aug. 31, 1930
Eugene Meyer	Sept. 16, 1930–May 10, 1933
Eugene R. Black	May 19, 1933–Aug. 15, 1934
Marriner S. Eccles	Nov. 15, 1934–Jan. 31, 1948
Thomas B. McCabe	April 15, 1948–March 31, 1951
William McChesney Martin, Jr.	April 2, 1951–Jan. 31, 1970
Arthur F. Burns	Feb. 1, 1970–Jan. 31, 1978
G. William Miller	Mar. 8, 1978–Aug. 6, 1979
Paul A. Volcker	Aug. 6, 1979–Aug. 11, 1987
Alan Greenspan	Aug. 11, 1987–

Bibliography

Adams, Earl W. "Thomas Bayard McCabe." In *Biographical Dictionary of the Board of Governors of the Federal Reserve*, ed. Bernard S. Katz. Westport CT: Greenwood, 1992. Pp. 166–72.

Ahene, Rexford. "Andrew Felton Brimmer." In *Biographical Dictionary of the Board of Governors of the Federal Reserve*, ed. Bernard S. Katz. Westport CT: Greenwood, 1992. Pp. 25–30.

All Bank Statistics, United States 1896–1955. Board of Governors of the Federal Reserve System, 1959.

Allsbrook, Ogden O. Jr. "Eugene R. Black." In *Biographical Dictionary of the Board of Governors of the Federal Reserve*, ed. Bernard Katz. Westport CT: Greenwood, 1992. Pp. 14–24.

Ascheim, Joseph. *Techniques of Monetary Control.* Baltimore MD: Johns Hopkins Press, 1961.

Ball, Laurence, and Robert R. Tchaidze. "The Fed and the New Economy." *American Economic Review,* May 2002.

Barber, William J. "Marriner Stoddard Eccles." In *Biographical Dictionary of the Board of Governors of the Federal Reserve*, ed. Bernard S. Katz. Westport CT: Greenwood, 1992. Pp.82–93.

Barro, Robert. "Is Alan Greenspan a Genius or Just Plain Lucky?" *Business Week,* August 16, 1999.

_____. "Rational Expectations and the Role of Monetary Policy," *Journal of Monetary Economics* 2 (1976) .

Bies, Susan Schmidt. "Managing Business Risks." Speech before the Oregon Bankers Association, June 16, 2003.

Blinder, Alan. "Is Government Too Political?" *Foreign Affairs*, Nov/Dec 1997.

_____. "Is the Fed Too Political?" *Foreign Affairs*, Nov/Dec 1997.

_____. *The Region.* Federal Reserve Bank of Minneapolis, December 1994.

Carlstrom, Charles T., and Timothy S. Fuerst. "The Taylor Rule: A Guidepost for Monetary Policy." *Review,* Federal Reserve Bank of Cleveland, July 2003.

Cicarelli, Juli. "Frederic Adrian Delano." In *Biographical Dictionary of the Board of Governors of the Federal Reserve,* ed. Bernard Katz. Westport CT: Greenwood, 1992. Pp. 114–21.

_____. "Nancy Hays Teeters." In *Biographical Dictionary of the Board of Governors of the Federal Reserve,* ed. Bernard S. Katz. Westport CT: Greenwood, 1992. Pp. 317–321.

Claypool, Gregory A. "Menc Stephen Szymczak", in Katz, op. cit., Pp. 316–318.

Connell, Michael. "Charles Sumner Hamlin." In *Biographical Dictionary of the Board of Governors of the Federal Reserve,* ed. Bernard S. Katz. Westport CT: Greenwood, 1992. Pp. 75–79.

Degen, Robert A. *The American Monetary System.* Lexington MA: D.C. Heath, 1987.

Dowd, Kevin. *The State and the Monetary System.* New York: St. Mary's Press, 1989.

Eccles, Marriner Stoddard "The Climax of the Treasury–Federal Reserve Dispute." In *Money and Economic Activity,* ed. Lawrence Ritter. New York: Houghton Mifflin, 1967.

Eckstein, Otto, and John Kareken. "The Bills Only Policy: A Summary of the Issues." In *Money and Economic Activity,* ed. Lawrence Ritter. Boston: Houghton Mifflin, 1967. Pp. 184–187.

Federal Deposit Insurance Corporation. *Annual Reports.* 1990–2001.

Federal Reserve Bulletin, 1993.

Ferguson, Roger W. Interview in *The Region.* Federal Reserve Bank of Minneapolis, June 2000.

Friedman, Benjamin. "Lessons on Monetary Policy from the 1980s." *Journal of Economic Perspectives,* Summer 1988.

Friedman, Milton. *A Program for Monetary Stability.* New York: Fordham University, 1959.

_____. "Rediscounting." *Money and Economic Activity,* ed. Lawrence Ritter. 3rd ed. Boston: Houghton Mifflin, 1967. Pp. 211–17.

_____, and Anna Schwartz. *A Monetary History of the United States, 1867–1960.* Princeton NJ: Princeton University Press, 1963.

_____, and _____. *Monetary Statistics of the United States.* New York: National Bureau of Economic Research, 1970.

Friedman, Milton, and Walter Heller. *Monetary vs. Fiscal Policy.* New York: W.W. Norton, 1969.

Galbraith, John Kenneth. "Administered Prices and Monetary-Fiscal Policy" In *Money and Economic Activity,* ed. Lawrence Ritter. 3rd ed. Boston: Houghton Mifflin, 1967. Pp. 317–324.

Gay, David E. R., and Thomas R. McKinnon. "William Wayne Sherrill." In *Biographical Dictionary of the Board of Governors of the Federal Reserve,* ed. Bernard S. Katz. Westport CT: Greenwood, 1992.

Gill, Richard T. *Economics and the Public Interest.* 5th ed. Mountain View CA: Mayfield, 1991.

Glasner, David. *Free Banking and Monetary Reform.* Cambridge: Cambridge University Press, 1989.

Goodhart, Charles. *The Evolution of Central Banks*. Cambridge: M.I.T. Press, 1988.

Gramlich, Edward M. Speech before the Allied Social Science Association, Washington, D.C., January 4, 2003.

_____. Speech before the Wharton Public Policy Forum, Philadelphia, April 22, 1999.

_____. Speech on Social Security Reform, Dec. 8, 1998.

Havrilesky, Thomas, and Bernard S. Katz. "Alan Greenspan." In *Biographical Dictionary of the Board of Governors of the Federal Reserve*, ed. Bernard S. Katz. Westport CT: Greenwood, 1992. Pp. 105–113.

Herren, Robert S. "Adolph Casper Miller," In *Biographical Dictionary of the Board of Gaevernors of the Federal Reserve*, ed. Bernard Katz. Westport CT: Greenwood, 1992, Pp.227–33.

_____. "Paul Moritz Warburg." In *Biographical Dictionary of the Board of Governors of the Federal Reserve*, ed. Bernard S. Katz. Westport CT: Greenwood, 1992. Pp. 349–355.

_____. "Paul Volcker." In *Biographical Dictionary of the Board of Governors of the Federal Reserve*, ed. Bernard S. Katz. Westport CT: Greenwood, 1992. Pp. 329–43.

Hoskins, W. Lee "Defending Zero Inflation." *Quarterly Review*, Federal Reserve Bank of Minneapolis, Spring 1991, Pp. 16–18.

James, John A. "The Conundrum of the Low Issue of National Banknotes." *Journal of Political Economy* 84 (April 1976): Pp. 359–67.

Journal of Monetary Economics, 1976, Pp. 1–26.

Judd, John, and Glen Rudebusch. "Taylor's Rule and the Fed, 1970–1997." Economic Review, Federal Reserve Bank of San Francisco, 1998.

Kapuria-Foreman, Vibha. "Roy Archibald Young." In *Biographical Dictionary of the Board of Governors of the Federal Reserve*, ed. Bernard Katz. Westport CT: Greenwood 1992. Pp. 359–72.

Katz, Bernard. "David W. Mullins, Jr." In *Biographical Dictionary of the Board of Governors of the Federal Reserve System,* ed. Bernard S. Katz. Westport CT: Greenwood, 1992.

Kugler, Penny. "Henry Wallich." In *Biographical Dictionary of the Board of Governors of the Federal Reserve,* ed. Bernard S. Katz. Westport CT: Greenwood, 1992. Pp. 246–348.

_____. "James L. Robertson." In *Biographical Dictionary of the Board of Governors of the Federal Reserve,* ed. Bernard S. Katz. Westport CT: Greenwood, 1992. Pp. 288–291.

_____. "Robert C. Holland." In *Biographical Dictionary of the Board of Governors of the Federal Reserve,* ed. Bernard S. Katz. Westport CT: Greenwood, 1992. Pp. 133–36.

Leahigh, David J. "Edmund Platt." In *Biographical Dictionary of the Board of Governors of the Federal Reserve,* ed. Bernard S. Katz. Westport CT: Greenwood, 1992. Pp.276–77.

Leijonhufvud, Axel. "Inflation and Economic Performance." In *Money in Crisis*, ed. Barry Siegal, Cambridge MA: Ballinger, 1984. Pp. 19–30.

Leon, Jean-Claude. "George Roosa James." In *Biographical Dictionary of the Board of Governors of the Federal Reserve*, ed. Bernard S. Katz. Westport CT: Greenwood, 1992. pp 143–45.

Lerner, Abba. "Inflationary Depression and the Regulation of Administered Prices." In *Money and Economic Activity*, ed. Lawrence Ritter. 3rd ed. Boston: Houghton Mifflin, 1967. Pp. 307–17.

Lindsey, Lawrence. "How to Grow Faster." Speech before the Federal Reserve Board, Oct. 11, 1996.

_____. Interview in *The Region*. Federal Reserve Bank of Minneapolis, March 1993.

Marshall, James N. "Eugene Meyer." In *Biographical Dictionary of the Board of Governors of the Federal Reserve*, ed. Bernard S. Katz. Westport CT: Greenwood, 1992. Pp. 211–26.

Mayor, Laurence H. Interview in *The Region*. Federal Reserve Bank of Minneapolis, September 1998.

McKinney, Marie "G. William Miller." In *Biographical Dictionary of the Board of Governors of the Federal Reserve*, ed. Bernard S. Katz. Westport CT: Greenwood, 1992. Pp. 234–44.

_____. "Lyle Gramley." In *Biographical Dictionary of the Board of Governors of the Federal Reserve*, ed. Bernard S. Katz. Westport CT: Greenwood, 1992. Pp. 100–104.

Meltzer, Alan. *A History of the Federal Reserve*. Vol I. Chicago: University of Chicago Press, 2003.

Meltzer, Yale L. "J. Dewey Daane." In *Biographical Dictionary of the Board of Governors of the Federal Reserve*, ed. Bernard S. Katz. Westport CT: Greenwood, 1992. Pp. 69–71.

Meyer, Annette E. "Preston Martin." In *Biographical Dictionary of the Board of Governors of the Federal Reserve*, ed. Bernard S. Katz. Westport CT: Greenwood, 1992. Pp. 186–91.

Miller, Roger LeRoy, and David D. VanHoose. *Modern Money and Banking*. 3rd Ed. New York: McGraw-Hill, 1993.

Mills, Geofrey T. "William Proctor Gould Harding." In *Biographical Dictionary of the Board of Governors of the Federal Reserve*, ed. Bernard S. Katz. Westport CT: Greenwood, 1992. Pp. 122–28.

Mulling, David W. Interview in *The Region*. Federal Reserve Bank of Minneapolis, September 1991.

Phillips, Susan M. Interview in *The Region*. Federal Reserve Bank of Minneapolis, March 1992.

Pierce, Thomas. "Jeffry Bucher." In *Biographical Dictionary of the Board of Governors of the Federal Reserve*, ed. Bernard S. Katz. Westport CT: Greenwood, 1992. Pp. 33–37.

Poole, William. "Lessons on Monetary Policy from the 1980s." *Journal of Economic Perspectives*, Summer 1988.

Prather, Charles L. *Money and Banking*. 9th ed. Homewood IL: Richard D. Irwin, 1969.

Robbins, Ronald. "Edward H. Cunningham." In *Biographical Dictionary of the Board of Governors of the Federal Reserve*, ed. Bernard S. Katz. Westport CT: Greenwood, 1992. Pp. 66–68.

Rothbard, Murray. *The Case Against the Fed*. Auburn, AL: The Ludwig von Mises Institute, 1994.

_____. "The Federal Reserve as a Cartelization Device." In *Money in Crisis*, ed. Barry Siegel. Cambridge MA: Ballinger, 1984.

Saltzman, Cynthia. "Wayland Wells Magee." In *Biographical Dictionary of the Board of Governors of the Federal Reserve*, ed. Bernard S. Katz. Westport CT: Greenwood, 1992. Pp. 179–80.

Samuelson, Paul. "Recent Monetary Controversy." In *Money and Economic Activity*, ed. Lawrence Ritter. 3d ed. Boston: Houghton Mifflin, 1967. Pp. 175–83.

_____, and Robert Solow. "Analytical Aspects of Anti-inflation Policy." Reprinted in Ritter, op. cit., Pp. 329–39.

Sargent, Thomas J., and Neil Wallace. "Rational Expectations and the Theory of Economic Policy." Federal Reserve Bank of Minneapolis. *Studies in Monetary Economics* 2 (June 1975), Pp. 1–19.

Schmotter, James W. "Daniel Richard Crissinger." In *Biographical Dictionary of the Board of Governors of the Federal Reserve*, ed. Bernard S. Katz. Westport CT: Greenwood, 1992. Pp. 60–65.

Selgin, George A. *The Theory of Free Banking*. Totowa, NJ: Rowman and Littlefield, 1988.

Simmons, Jane M. "Sherman Maisel." In *Biographical Dictionary of the Board of Governors of the Federal Reserve*, ed. Bernard S. Katz. Westport CT: Greenwood, 1992. Pp. 181–85.

Slichter, Sumner H. "How Bad is Inflation?" In *Money and Economic Activity*, ed. Lawrence Ritter. 3d ed. Boston: Houghton Mifflin, 1967. Pp. 324–28.

Smith, Vera C. *The Rationale of Central Banking*. Westminster, England: P.S. King & Son, 1936.

Sternlight, Peter D., and Robert Lindsay. "The Significance and Limitations of Free Reserves." In *Money and Economic Activity*, ed. Lawrence Ritter. 3d ed. Boston: Houghton Mifflin, 1967. Pp. 169–75.

Taylor, John. *Inflation, Unemployment and Monetary Policy*. Cambridge MA: M.I.T. Press, 1998.

Thronborrow, Nancy M. "C. Candy Balderston." In *Biographical Dictionary of the Board of Governors of the Federal Reserve*, ed. Bernard S. Katz. Westport CT: Greenwood, 1992. Pp. 8–13.

_____. "John Keown McKee." In *Biographical Dictionary of the Board of Governors of the Federal Reserve*, ed. Bernard S. Katz. Westport CT: Greenwood, 1992. Pp. 173–78.

Thornton, Daniel L., and David C. Wheelock. "A History of the Asymmetric Policy Directive." *Review*, Federal Reserve Bank of St. Louis, 2000.

Bibliography

Timberlake, Richard H. Jr., "The Central Banking Role of Clearinghouse Associations." *Journal of Money Credit and Banking* 16 (February 1984): Pp. 1–16.

Toma, Mark. Review of *Charting Twentieth Century Monetary Policy: Herbert Hoover and Benjamin Strong, 1917–1927* by Silvano A. Wueschner. Economic History Services, Oct. 25, 2000, www.ehnet.bookreviews/library/0307.shtml.

Vencill, Daniel. "William McChesney Martin." In *Biographical Dictionary of the Board of Governors of the Federal Reserve,* ed. Bernard S. Katz. Westport CT: Greenwood, 1992. Pp. 192–209.

Wallace, Neil. "Microeconomic Theories of Macroeconomic Phenomena and their Implications for Monetary Policy." Federal Reserve Bank of Minneapolis, *Studies in Monetary Economics* 3 (December 1977): Pp. 23–33.

Wells, Donald R. "Banking Before the Federal Reserve." *The Freeman* 37 (June 1987): Pp. 231–35.

_____. "The Free Banking Model Applied to Pre-1914 Canadian Banking." *Studies in Economic Analysis* 12, no. 2 (Fall 1989): Pp. 3–21.

_____. "Money's Ability to Manage Itself: Evidence from Canada During the Great Depression of the 1930s." *Journal of Economics and Finance* 13, Pp. 171–77.

_____. "The Reaction of the American and Canadian Banking Systems to the Panic of 1907." *The Journal of Economics* XIII (1987): Pp. 67–73.

_____. "Rudolph Martin Evans." In *Biographical Dictionary of the Board of Governors of the Federal Reserve,* ed. Bernard S. Katz. Westport CT: Greenwood, 1992. Pp. 91–93.

Wells, Donald R., and L. S. Scruggs. "Emergency Currency and the 1914 Banking Crisis: Implications for Financial Deregulation." *Studies in Economic Analysis* 10, no. 2 (Fall 1986):

_____, and _____. "Historical Insights into the Deregulation of Money and Banking." *The Cato Journal* 5 (Winter 1986): Pp. 899–910.

_____, and _____. "An Historical Review of Insurance of Bank Deposits." *Mid-South Journal of Economics,* 8 no. 3 (1984): Pp. 467–68.

White, Jack B. "Edward W. Kelley." In *Biographical Dictionary of the Board of Governors of the Federal Reserve,* ed. Bernard S. Katz. Westport CT: Greenwood, 1992. Pp. 151–53.

_____. "John P. LaWare." In *Biographical Dictionary of the Board of Governors of the Federal Reserve,* ed. Bernard S. Katz. Westport CT: Greenwood, 1992. Pp. 158–160.

White, Lawrence H. *Competition and Currency.* New York: New York University Press, 1989.

Willes, Mark H. "Eliminating Policy Surprises: An Inexpensive Way to Beat Inflation." Federal Reserve Bank of Minneapolis *Annual Report,* 1978.

_____. "Rational Expectations — Fresh Ideas That Challenge Some Established Views of Policy Making." Federal Reserve Bank of Minneapolis *Annual Report,* 1977.

Winder, Robert C. "Manuel H. Johnson." In In *Biographical Dictionary of the Board of Governors of the Federal Reserve,* ed. Bernard S. Katz. Westport CT: Greenwood, 1992. Pp. 146–50.

_____. "Martha Romayne Segar." In In *Biographical Dictionary of the Board of Governors of the Federal Reserve,* ed. Bernard S. Katz. Westport CT: Greenwood, 1992. Pp. 295–99.

_____. "Wayne D. Angell." In In *Biographical Dictionary of the Board of Governors of the Federal Reserve,* ed. Bernard S. Katz. Westport CT: Greenwood, 1992. Pp. 3–7.

Wood, J. Stuart "Capital Formation in the United States and the Question of a Capital Shortage." In *Money in Crisis,* ed. Barry Siegel. Cambridge MA: Ballinger, 1984. Pp. 73–86.

Yeager, Leland. "The Medium of Exchange." In *Readings in Monetary Theory,* ed. Robert W. Clower. Baltimore MD: Penguin, 1969.

Yellen, Janet. Interview in *The Region.* Federal Reserve Bank of Minneapolis, June 1995.

Index

211

Index